Secession Winter

The Marcus Cunliffe Lecture Series
JAROD ROLL, SERIES EDITOR

Secession Winter

When the Union Fell Apart

ROBERT J. COOK
WILLIAM L. BARNEY
ELIZABETH R. VARON

Johns Hopkins University Press
Baltimore

© 2013 Johns Hopkins University Press
All rights reserved. Published 2013
Printed in the United States of America on acid-free paper
2 4 6 8 9 7 5 3

Johns Hopkins University Press
2715 North Charles Street
Baltimore, Maryland 21218-4363
www.press.jhu.edu

Library of Congress Cataloging-in-Publication Data

Cook, Robert J., 1958–
Secession winter : when the Union fell apart / Robert J. Cook, William L. Barney, Elizabeth R. Varon.
p. cm. — (The Marcus Cunliffe lecture series)
Includes bibliographical references and index.
ISBN 978-1-4214-0895-8 (hardcover : alk. paper) — ISBN 978-1-4214-0896-5 (pbk. : alk. paper) — ISBN 978-1-4214-0897-2 (electronic) — ISBN 1-4214-0895-3 (hardcover : alk. paper) — ISBN 1-4214-0896-1 (pbk. : alk. paper) — ISBN 1-4214-0897-X (electronic)
1. Secession—Southern States. 2. Confederate States of America—Politics and government. 3. United States—History—Civil War, 1861–1865—Causes. 4. Slavery—Southern States—History—19th century. 5. Lee, Robert E. (Robert Edward), 1807–1870. 6. Collective memory—Southern States. I. Barney, William L. II. Varon, Elizabeth R., 1963– III. Title.
E459.C76 2013
973.7′13—dc23   2012027076

A catalog record for this book is available from the British Library.

Special discounts are available for bulk purchases of this book. For more information, please contact Special Sales at 410-516-6936 or specialsales@press.jhu.edu.

Johns Hopkins University Press uses environmentally friendly book materials, including recycled text paper that is composed of at least 30 percent post-consumer waste, whenever possible.

CONTENTS

Foreword vii
JAROD ROLL

Introduction: The Secession Crisis as a Study in Conflict Resolution   1
ROBERT J. COOK

Rush to Disaster: Secession and the Slaves' Revenge   10
WILLIAM L. BARNEY

"Save in Defense of My Native State": A New Look at Robert E. Lee's Decision to Join the Confederacy   34
ELIZABETH R. VARON

The Shadow of the Past: Collective Memory and the Coming of the American Civil War   58
ROBERT J. COOK

Conclusion: Conflicted Minds and Civil War Causation   86
ROBERT J. COOK

Notes   91
Guide to Further Reading   105
Index   113

FOREWORD

✤

The Marcus Cunliffe Centre for the Study of the American South was founded in 2007 to facilitate cutting-edge research and dialogue on the history of the Southern United States. Based at the University of Sussex in Brighton, England, the centre honors Marcus Cunliffe, Professor of American Studies at the University of Sussex from 1965 to 1980. Professor Cunliffe authored more than a dozen books that ranged across the disciplines of history, literature, and politics and did much to create and advance the interdisciplinary approach to understanding America's attachments across the Atlantic. Whether he wrote of the institutional presidency or of George Washington's human and monumental record, of wage work and chattel slavery, of literary history or the history of property rights, Cunliffe's work always sought to bridge disciplinary boundaries and raise challenging questions about issues at the heart of the American experience that spoke to popular as well as academic audiences.

In the spirit of this tradition, the Marcus Cunliffe Centre hosts the annual Cunliffe Lecture Series, which brings together in the United Kingdom the very best scholars in the field to comment on critical issues in the Southern past. These lectures are not intended to be exhaustive in scale or scope, but they do provide novel and incisive interpretations of contentious subjects. Like Professor Cunliffe's work, this lecture series aims to pose challenging questions and thus throw open fresh debates that will engage a broad audience of readers. To learn more and to follow the progress of the series, please visit our website: www.sussex.ac.uk/cunliffe.

Jarod Roll
Director
Marcus Cunliffe Centre
for the Study of the American South
University of Sussex

Secession Winter

ROBERT J. COOK

Introduction

❦

The Secession Crisis as a Study in Conflict Resolution

FOR FIVE MONTHS DURING the winter of 1860–61, the fate of the United States hung in the balance. Abraham Lincoln's election as president on November 6 precipitated a full-blown secession crisis. By the beginning of February, seven slave states of the Deep South had passed formal ordinances severing their connections with the American republic, founded at Philadelphia less than three-quarters of a century previously. Angry and frustrated, excited and fearful, ordinary Americans watched as a series of portentous events unfolded before them. None of them could know for certain that civil war was imminent, but many suspected the worst. Some on both sides of the Mason-Dixon line spent the winter hoping against hope for a sectional compromise that would secure lasting peace between North and South. Others were spoiling for a fight. Not a few, shaken to the core by their country's rapid descent into political chaos, simply struggled to comprehend what was happening.

Benjamin Brown French, a New Hampshire–born public servant who kept a diary for most of his adult life, was a keen observer of mid-nineteenth-century political life. Even he found it difficult to respond coherently to what was happening in this confusing period. A conservative Republican fortunate enough to receive a government appointment under the Lincoln administration, French privately greeted the news of South Carolina's impending secession with the thought that this act "would be the ruin of the State ... We must all wait coming events, and make the best of what may 'turn up.'" He was, he avowed, "an ultra Union man" who was for "concession & conciliation" and "utterly opposed to any intermeddling with Southern rights." Incumbent president James Buchanan's weak response to what quickly proved to be a disunion bandwagon soon altered French's position. On January 1 he railed against the "hotheaded traitors" seeking to sunder the Union and bemoaned the absence of a strong executive like his hero Andrew Jackson, who had faced down South Carolina disunionists during the nullification crisis of 1832–33.[1]

A month later Benjamin French was anticipating peace as a Virginia-backed convention began deliberating compromise measures in Washington. Another week went by, and his fragile optimism had already begun to evaporate. The rebels' seizure of federal property across the South induced him to put his faith in an otherworldly power. "What the end is to be no one knows—" he confided in his diary, "but as God orders all things right, I have no doubt this seeming 'partial evil' will result in 'universal good!' We must wait patiently & prayerfully, do *our* duty & *Trust*! The end must come!" That end finally came in April when President Lincoln requested a military response to the Confederates' bombardment of government-held Fort Sumter in Charleston harbor. French was downcast. "Awful times!" he wrote in his diary on April 19, "Civil war all around us." He still hoped it might be possible to allow the seceding states to leave the Union peacefully. Another four states, all in the Upper South, joined the Confederacy in the weeks that followed. But by then the die was cast. Northerners and Southerners were already girding themselves for war. It would be four grim years before the Union was restored— in a very different form from the one around which millions of Americans, French included, rallied in the spring of 1861.[2]

Rather than focusing on the hoary issue of whether civil war was inevitable—the traditional line of enquiry for much scholarship on the secession crisis—this book investigates the causal relationship between internal divisions of all kinds, the inherently political process of secession, and the outbreak of the Civil War. It limns both the multiplicity of inner conflicts that wracked Americans during this crisis and the disparate actions that those same divided Americans took to resolve them—actions that led directly to the bloodiest war in U.S. history. Importantly, each of the three contributors acknowledges the central role played by politics in the secession crisis but avoids the temptation to view politics as simply a party affair. Much recent work on the Civil War era demonstrates the racial, class, and gender dimensions of political struggle in this era: not just formal political struggle involving parties and elections but also societal power relations between whites and nonwhites, elites and masses, and men and women. Highly charged political rhetoric in the winter of 1860–61 dripped with meanings embedded in these relationships. Secessionists exhorted their fellow Southerners to act like men and to defend their women and children from the impending ravages of lustful blacks whose civilizing chains would be cut by barbarous Yankee abolitionists. Republicans, meanwhile, implored Northerners to resist the siren call of compromise and stand up manfully against the challenge posed by treacherous "plantocrats." Rhetoric like this was intended to mobilize all manner of groups and individuals behind the leadership of sectional politicians. It aimed to do so by finessing internal conflicts and promoting the unity of North and South in the face of a demonstrable external threat.

What historian Henry Brooks Adams called "the Great Secession Winter" can be viewed in terms of five linked and largely overlapping phases. First, the secession of the cotton states in late 1860 and early 1861 resulted in the creation of an avowedly independent Confederate government in early February. Second, the immediate response by shocked Americans in the North and the nonseceding slave states of the Upper South to the reality of secession prompted calls for coercive federal action as well as feverish compromise efforts inside and outside Congress. Third, attempts were made by Senator, later U.S. Secretary of State, William H. Seward in the early months of 1861 to instigate a practical peace policy that would stimulate the reconstruction of the Union by maintaining the loyalty of whites in the

Upper South. Fourth, an increasingly tense policy debate, North and South, ensued over the fate of the few military installations in Confederate territory that remained in the hands of the United States. This debate came to a head when President Lincoln decided in late March to resupply the federal garrison at Fort Sumter—a decision that terminally undermined Seward's peace efforts by forcing the hand of the Confederate government. Fifth, following the Confederates' attack on Sumter and the garrison's surrender on April 13, Lincoln called upon the individual states for troops to suppress what he and most Northerners now regarded as a rebellion against national authority. His proclamation prompted a second wave of secession among the slave states of the Upper South: Virginia, North Carolina, Arkansas, and Tennessee all left the Union. Benjamin French's lingering hopes of a bloodless resolution of the conflict proved to be a mere chimera.[3]

The fundamental conflict, of course, lay between North and South. Politicians from the two inchoate sections had been at loggerheads since 1819 when Northerners in Congress made concerted attempts to prevent the admission of Missouri as a slave state (efforts that resulted in the prohibition of slavery above the new Missouri Compromise line of 36°30′). Contemporaries agreed and modern historians concur that Southern slavery was the root cause of the growing sectional divide, though there was, and is, considerable debate about why this was the case. After showing signs of dying out in the early years of the republic (it had virtually disappeared from the Northern "free" states by 1830), slavery flourished in the staple-producing regions of the Deep South. On the eve of the Civil War nearly 4 million African Americans worked as bonded laborers in the slave states. The backbreaking toil of the enslaved made some white men very rich. It also molded a region whose social structure, politics, ideology, and culture were heavily determined by the existence of the "peculiar institution."

The fact that North and South proceeded to wage war against each other for four years obscures the many internal divisions that beset the people of these two vast regions, before, during, and after the secession crisis. Without some understanding of these divisions and an awareness of how contemporaries tried to eradicate them, the outbreak of the American Civil War in the spring of 1861 makes little sense. Modern neo-Confederate activists might like to think that Southerners fought the Civil War as an undivided people (they would certainly like others to think so), but the historical record suggests otherwise. White Southerners were profoundly conflicted in the late 1850s. Living in a patriarchal slave society touched by the rapid advance of modern capitalism generated enormous psychological strains and social tensions. Southern radicals sought to resolve these debilitating internal divisions through revolution. Secession, they insisted, would liberate the Southern people from Yankee criticism and meddling, which they believed not only dishonored the South but also threatened it with disaster. They posited a bright new future for Southerners in an independent slaveholding nation whose material strength would attract respect from European powers like Great Britain and France. For whites who believed their way of life, their very lives even, to be imperiled by the election of an antislavery Northern president, this was an enticing vision.

The opening essay in this book, William L. Barney's "Rush to Disaster: Secession and the Slaves' Revenge," delves deep into the dark heart of the South's inner conflict over race. He does so by posing a fundamental question about the secession of the cotton states. Why did pro-slavery radicals take a leap of faith in the winter of 1860–61—a leap intended to secure the South's peculiar institution but, irony of Southern ironies, one that led to its destruction as a result of military defeat at the hands of the Union army? He finds the answer in white anxiety, fear, even guilt over the holding of slaves. Secession, contends Barney, provided Southern whites with an opportunity to regain their self-respect and restore social harmony, both of which were threatened directly by the Black Republicans' sudden ascent to national power.

William Barney's essay highlights a major fault line within the South: that pertaining between the Upper and Lower South, the former a geographically diverse region in which 67 percent of Southern whites resided. Serious doubts about the wisdom and morality of slaveholding, Barney contends, persisted in the Upper South to a greater extent than they did in the cotton states. States like Virginia and Kentucky with significant urban centers possessed closer economic ties to the North as well as more robust competition between political parties. The Appalachian Mountains chain was home to many non-slaveholding whites who had long resented the material and political power of planter elites within their respective states. Affection for the Union, though by no means fully extinguished in the cotton states, was significantly greater in the Upper South, not least in Virginia, the home of Washington, Jefferson, Madison, and other members of the republic's founding generation. These emotional ties to the Union, internal social divisions, and the residual strength of the old Whig Party (long a force for conservatism and nationalism in the United States) presented the proponents of compromise with an opportunity. William Seward and other leading political figures believed they could save the Union and stave off civil war if they could prevent the Upper South from joining the Confederacy.[4]

Elizabeth R. Varon's essay, "'Save in Defense of My Native State': A New Look at Robert E. Lee's Decision to Join the Confederacy," reveals that these hopes were not entirely illusory. For the duration of the secession crisis, the man who would become the Confederacy's most effective military commander was genuinely uncertain over how to respond to events. In common with many of the South's conditional Unionists during this period, Lee was deeply conflicted. Varon's account of how he resolved his personal dilemmas eschews traditional explanations. Lee did not just side with his native state because of some innate attachment to Virginia and the South. Instead, she argues, his decision was rational and calculated. He was pushed belatedly into the Southern camp by a mounting conviction that the Republicans had not paid due respect to Virginia's historic paramountcy within the republic and pulled into it by canny tactics on the part of those politicians who wanted him to command the state's military forces. Varon concludes that while Lee's inner crisis was resolved primarily by Lincoln's decision to "coerce" the Deep

South states back into the Union, his own decision to secede expressly out of loyalty to his native Virginia should be seen not only as a slap in the face of the antislavery Republicans but also as an implicit criticism of rash secessionists.

Initially, Northerners were no more united in their response to the crisis than Southern whites. This was hardly surprising. The North was a rapidly industrializing, aggressively capitalistic society riven by numerous tensions generated by market penetration, western expansion, urbanization, and European immigration. The section's dominant Republicans sought to unify Northerners behind their own leadership by vaunting the superiority of free labor and denigrating Southern slavery as economically and morally retrograde. Two-party competition remained healthy in most parts of the North in the late 1850s. Established partisan loyalties therefore did much to condition the way Northerners responded individually and collectively to the secession crisis. Although many Republicans, perhaps a majority of party leaders and activists, were prepared from the beginning to force seceding states back into the Union, Democrats like Stephen A. Douglas proved far more willing to explore the possibilities of a compromise solution to the crisis. Lincoln's decision to reprovision Fort Sumter resulted, in part at least, from his determination to resolve the internal conflicts of his own section: the need to hold his own party together and to secure the support of Northern Democrats for a war to save the Union.[5]

Robert J. Cook's "The Shadow of the Past: Collective Memory and the Coming of the American Civil War" contends that the past was a source of both internal division and conflict resolution during the secession crisis. He shows how politicians across the fractured American republic constructed sectionally unifying grievance narratives to convince Northerners and Southerners of the rightness of their respective causes. One of the secessionists' main tasks, he suggests, was to break the deeply felt historical ties that bound white Southerners to the Union while simultaneously building a new proslavery nation on the foundations laid by statesmen like Washington and Jefferson. They did so by grafting a highly selective account of the North's alleged thirty years war against slavery onto Southerners' historically informed interpretation of the American Revolution as the genesis of a constitutional Union that bolstered slavery. Northern Republicans, on the other hand, developed their own potent grievance narrative that cast themselves as the heirs of the founders and their enemies as the agents of the "Slave Power" and traitors to the glorious legacy of 1776.

Many Americans breathed a sigh of relief when war finally came. As the Republican senator John Sherman of Ohio put it after the Confederate attack on Fort Sumter had electrified the North, "Civil war is actually upon us & strange to say it brings a feeling of relief—the suspense is over." Statements like this should send a chill down the spines of modern readers. We know what Sherman and his contemporaries did not: that the ensuing bloodbath (in which his brother William was to play a considerable part) resulted in the deaths of at least 750,000 combatants. They make more sense, however, if we acknowledge the degree to which the outbreak of war not only ended the suspense of the previous five months but also resolved—or at least promised to resolve—the many internal conflicts on display during the winter of 1860–61: not only the primary conflict between North and South but also white Southerners' internal divisions engendered by the fact that they dwelt amidst a race of people who wanted to be free and Northerners' own divisions, including partisan disagreements over whether a compromise solution could be found to the secession crisis.[6]

As noted above, scholarly debate over that crisis has often centered on the issue of whether war could have been averted. David Potter argued as long ago as 1942 that compromise efforts might have been successful if Republicans had taken Southern secession more seriously from the start. This thesis was rejected eight years later by Kenneth M. Stampp, who contended that most Republicans were resolved to put slavery on the road to extinction and that therefore war between North and South was virtually inevitable in 1861. The contributors to this volume recognize the importance of contingent events to the outcome of the secession crisis. In the final analysis, however, it seems clear that compromise efforts—most notably Senator John J. Crittenden's ill-fated plan to extend the Missouri Compromise line to the Pacific Ocean and protect slavery below that line in all current and future U.S. territory—did not offer to resolve effectively the inter- and intra-sectional conflicts bedeviling Americans at this crossroads in their history. Secession and war, by contrast, appeared to give the people of both sections greater hope in this respect. We can only speculate whether they would have made different decisions had they known the appalling human cost they were about to pay.[7]

WILLIAM L. BARNEY

Rush to Disaster
❧
Secession and the Slaves' Revenge

THIS ESSAY EXPLORES THE critical question of why the secessionists plunged the South into disaster in the winter of 1860–61 by insisting on breaking up the Union, a course of action that conservatives across the South, including many large planters, decried as a rash act that would provoke a civil war and destroy, and very quickly at that, the institution of slavery the secessionists professed to be defending.[1] Any answer to this question must begin with the presence of millions of enslaved African Americans in the South, a presence that had a profound impact on the thinking and perceptions of Southern whites. More specifically, this essay argues that every action, gesture, and expression of the slaves that spoke to their humanity and yearning to be free elicited from Southern whites patterns of denial, repression, and projection that so distorted their perception of reality, especially in the case of rabid secessionists, that whites in the Lower South ignored all the risks involved and rushed to embrace secession in the winter of 1860–61.[2] This was the slaves' revenge. By daily reaffirming their humanity, they heightened the unease, in some cases guilt, whites felt in owning slaves and increased their sensitivity to outside condemnation to the point where only secession seemed to offer a release from all that troubled them.[3] Virtually all Southern whites felt the sting of abolitionist attacks, but only diehard secessionists found these moral condemnations to be literally intolerable, an unconscionable affront to their whole sense of self.

That a precipitous withdrawal from the Union following Lincoln's election would be suicidal for the slave interests of the South was readily apparent to former Whigs and many, perhaps most, of the wealthy, established planters. They denounced such a course of action as "madness" and "insanity" and foresaw, in the words of James C. Johnston, one of North Carolina's wealthiest planters, either "the most wretched anarchy or the most horrible & bloody civil war that ever was recorded in history."[4] Secession, warned Benjamin F. Perry, a leading Unionist in South Carolina's upcountry, would unleash "all the horrors of civil war and revolution."[5]

Speaking for the city's commercial community, the *New Orleans Bee* echoed the sentiments of conservatives in the South when it insisted on November 12, 1860, that fanatical secessionists had blown completely out of proportion the threat posed by Lincoln's election. "Lincoln will be the most powerless President ever inaugurated," the paper declared. "He will have to contend with a hostile majority in both houses of Congress ... Every nomination made by him will be subjected to rigid scrutiny, and if tainted with sectionalism will be unceremoniously rejected." Three days later, the editor proclaimed that unless Southern congressmen were so foolish as to walk out, there was "no possibility whatever of the slightest aggression by Congress on the South." Surely, a prudent policy of consultation among the slave states and a willingness to judge the Republicans by their actions were preferable to embracing disunion, "an uncertain and perilous remedy" for alleged wrongs. After all, as a letter writer using the ironic pseudonym "State Rights" reasoned: "If we are incapable of maintaining our rights *in* the Union, are not our resources palpably inadequate to their maintenance *out* of the Union, with the power of our enemies largely augmented by the removal of those constitutional restraints which now keep them partially in check?"[6]

In South Carolina, where secession fever burned hottest, the large slaveholding interests outside the overwhelmingly black plantation districts in the low country initially counseled delay until assurances of cooperation were received from other states. Such was the advice of the planter James Henry Hammond, then serving in the U.S. Senate.[7] A firebrand earlier in his career, Hammond had moderated his views by the 1850s. His grudging acceptance of the North's growing material strength and his fear that any premature move to secede would only enable demagogic politicians to throw the South into chaos led him to conclude that the best and safest course was to present a united front and maintain Southern rights within the Union. Such views were anathema to the state's fire-eaters, and they denounced Hammond as a traitor to the cause of Southern liberties. Unlike many of the radicals, including Charleston editor Robert Barnwell Rhett, Hammond was not an evangelical. He used a biblical defense of slavery for its tactical value against the abolitionists, but he never internalized the religious values of the evangelical defenders of slavery. As he put it, the evangelical message "fell upon me like dew on the desert sands."[8] He accepted no limits on the exercise of his will alone. The ruthless pursuit of power defined his life. Along the way he nearly ruined his political career by sexually molesting the young daughters of Wade Hampton II, and he did ruin his marriage by openly humiliating his wife when he fathered children by a slave mistress and perhaps her daughter as well. He was an unrepentant sinner under no illusions that a God of saving grace looked kindly upon him and his actions. "God hates *me*," he wrote in his diary in 1854. "No wonder the Bible pourtrays him as a God full of Wrath, exacting the pound of flesh *and the blood*, since he has the *power*. No wonder Christian Preachers proclaim him as an infuriated Demon seeking whom he may destroy. Such and such only is my experience of him."[9] Having spent a lifetime bullying others, it was only natural for Hammond to think that God would do the same to him.

Once Lincoln's election was confirmed, the secessionists moved with astonishing speed. Within forty-eight hours they had orchestrated an outburst of popular enthusiasm for secession of such force that Hammond and other Unionist-leaning planters concluded that only by hopping onto the secessionist bandwagon could they hope to manage a revolution that was threatening to get out of control and leave them behind. Upon learning that his fellow senator, James Chesnut, had resigned his seat, Hammond immediately joined him. In explaining his decision and the rash of resignations of state and federal officials, Hammond drew on a metaphor that perfectly captured the psychological underpinnings of the urge to secede: "It reminds me of the Japanese who when insulted rip open their own bowels."[10] Rather than bear the brunt of any more Yankee insults, the secessionists would embrace the risk of seeing slavery eviscerated in a war for independence.

Doubts over Slavery

South Carolina's launching of the secession movement exposed the basic regional fault line of the slave South, that between the Upper and Lower South. It was a division that emerged in the first half of the nineteenth century and it followed patterns of soil types and isothermal lines on a map that demarcated areas, primarily in the Lower South, where the plantation crops of rice, sugar, and cotton could be grown for export markets. Percentages of white ownership of slaves and of slaves in the total population in the Upper South were roughly half those found in the Lower or cotton South. Politically, the division manifested itself in the continued vitality of the Whig Party in the Upper South years after the Whigs had been all but absorbed by the Democrats in the states that would comprise the first wave of secession. Ideologically and religiously, the division expressed itself in sharply contrasting, and understudied, moral attitudes toward slavery.[11] Although most whites in the Upper South accepted slavery as a vital economic institution that had to be defended, they also decried slavery as a moral wrong that gradually should be eliminated in Southern society. They looked forward to the day when the South would be rid of both slaves and free blacks through programs of gradual emancipation and the colonization of freed slaves outside of the United States. This was the position on slavery that Henry Clay, the South's most influential Whig, held until his death in 1852. As he explained his views in a letter of 1835 to William Henry Russell of Kentucky: "That slavery is unjust & is a great evil are undisputed axioms. The difficulty always has been how to get rid of it."[12] Robert J. Breckinridge, an Old School Presbyterian minister in Kentucky and a fellow antislavery gradualist, summarized the position of the colonizationists when he denounced slavery at the 1849 Kentucky Constitutional Convention as "this most atrocious of all human institutions."[13]

Despite the great conservative reaction that swept the South after Nat Turner's 1831 rebellion in Virginia and the onset of the abolitionist movement, pro-slavery advocates never succeeded in eliminating widespread doubts over the morality of slavery or efforts to rid the region of the institution. As politicians in the Upper South backed off from publicly espousing colonization, preachers assumed leadership of the movement. In the 1850s, Baptist and Old School Presbyterian ministers in Tennessee and Kentucky continued to take public stands against slavery and to condemn it as a moral evil. Among the most outspoken was James M. Pendleton, a native Virginian who pastored Baptist churches in Kentucky before his appointment as professor of theology at Union University in Murfreesboro, Tennessee. He wrote twenty articles for the *Examiner*, an antislavery newspaper in Louisville, and boldly declared himself "A Southern Emancipationist." He called for gradual emancipation through an expanded use of manumissions and the subsequent colonization of the freed slaves in Liberia. The editor of the *Alabama Baptist* denounced him in 1855 as a dangerous abolitionist for espousing such views and declared that he was utterly unfit to teach the young men of the South.[14]

Elsewhere in the Upper South, clerical critics of slavery, including some who once had been among the staunchest defenders of the institution, continued to be heard in the 1850s. Richard Fuller, a slaveholding Baptist minister in Beaufort, South Carolina, who was instrumental in the formation of the Southern Baptist Convention in 1845, defended slavery as an expression of divine will in a published exchange of letters with the Reverend Francis Wayland, president of Brown University. Rejecting Wayland's assertion that slavery was a sin, Fuller insisted that "what God sanctioned in the Old Testament, and permitted in the New, cannot be sin."[15] In 1847, and perhaps because his views on slavery were beginning to change, Fuller left South Carolina to assume the pastorship of the Seventh Baptist Church in Baltimore. Speaking before the American Colonization Society in 1851, he urged slaveholders to recognize that "slavery is not a good thing, and a thing to be perpetuated."[16] In due time, he believed, God's grace would dissolve the master-slave relationship and prepare the way for freed slaves to carry the gospel to Africa. An apostate in the eyes of his former followers in South Carolina, Fuller never did regain the stature and prestige he had enjoyed before his apparent change of heart regarding slavery.

The Upper South harbored not only defectors from slavery's erstwhile defenders but also persistent pockets of whites who questioned the idea that slavery was both a moral and economic good. The Reverend Dr. William A. Smith, one of Virginia's most outspoken pro-slavery advocates, reported back to Governor Henry A. Wise from a speaking tour in 1857 that "a secret suspicion of the morality of African slavery in the South" bothered "many of our best citizens." Most worrisome of all were the white workers in Portsmouth and Norfolk, "nine-tenths" of whom, according to Smith, were "abolitionists" who "would vote the slaves out of Virginia tomorrow" if they could be assured that the slaves would be expelled from the state.[17] In St. Louis, Louisville, and other manufacturing centers in the Upper South, antislavery sentiments were pervasive enough in the 1850s to keep alive support for gradual emancipation and to provide a voting base for fledgling Republican Party organizations.[18]

Pro-slavery forces in the Lower South were more successful in shutting down any public expression of doubts over slavery, but even here they could never rest easy. John Slidell, the Democratic Party boss of New Orleans, informed President James Buchanan that in the election of 1860 "seven eighths at least of the votes for Douglas were cast by the Irish & Germans, who are at heart abolitionists."[19] These immigrant workers could be excused for their antislavery leanings for, as a Louisiana editor noted, they "come from Nations where Slavery is not allowed, and they drink in abolition sentiments from their mothers' breasts; they entertain an utter abhorrence of being put on a level with blacks, whether in the field or in the workshop."[20] But what of those to the manor born, elite native-born whites who enjoyed all the privileges that the ownership of slaves could bestow? Caroline Pettigrew, mistress of her husband's Bonarva plantation in eastern North Carolina, wrote in 1856 that for all the misery of the poor in the North, "instances occur of horrible oppression & crime at the South . . . that could only be in the midst of slavery."[21] As secession excitement bordering on hysteria swirled around him in the days after Lincoln's election, her husband, Charles, confided to Caroline his fear that Southern whites as a people "must have committed some dreadful sins against the negro race, for which we are to be justly punished by a God of justice."[22]

In a rare admission to an outsider, the Louisiana sugar planter Richard Taylor declared in 1853 to his Northern visitor, Frederick Law Olmsted, that he viewed slavery "to be a very great evil, morally and economically. It was a curse upon the South . . . nothing would be more desirable than its removal, if it were possible to be accomplished."[23] Taylor was echoing the sentiments of a neighboring Creole planter. Also admitting slavery to be a moral wrong, the Creole lamented that "we could not do away with it if we wished; our duty is only . . . to lessen its evils as much as we can do so." Needless to say, both planters were also echoing the views of their slaves. Revealing an unusual degree of trust in a white man, William, one of Taylor's house slaves, responded to Olmsted's careful questioning by confiding that among themselves the plantation slaves were always talking about their desire to be free and to hire out their own labor.[24] Here, in a shared denunciation of slavery, was a source of agreement between planter and slave that the master was unable ever to acknowledge, let alone act upon.

In the privacy of their journals and diaries, the wives of the planter class expressed their moral qualms over slavery.[25] What galled many was the humiliation of living in the midst of mulatto children fathered by their close male kin. Ella Clanton Thomas, a planter's wife in Georgia, was prompted to write a long journal entry on miscegenation in January 1859 by her reaction to the child of a female house slave, a child "as white as any white child." Evidence of racial intermixing, she noted, was commonplace: the young mulatto women advertised in the newspapers as "Fancy girls" so as to attract a premium price in the slave market, the openness with which white men lived with their mulatto slaves, the concubines kept by planters, and the whiteness of far too many of the slaves around her. She blurted out: "Southern women are I believe all at heart abobisionists [sic]" and concluded that "slavery degrades the white man more than the Negro and oh exerts a most deleterious effect upon our children."[26] More famously, Mary Chesnut proclaimed in her subsequently published journal: "God forgive us, but ours is a *monstrous* system and wrong and inequity."[27]

To be sure, the Ella Thomases and Mary Chesnuts of the South were not crypto-abolitionists: the prerogatives of elite status trumped any moral reservations over slavery. And planters such as Charles Pettigrew and Richard Taylor who had strong moral doubts over slavery usually kept their opinions within the family. But the unease these members of the planter class expressed over slavery was representative enough of white opinion to be a source of chronic concern both to pro-slavery evangelicals and to secular defenders of slavery. The primary audience for the religious defense of slavery consisted not of the abolitionists, reviled throughout the South as heretical fanatics not open to reason, but Southern whites who might yet be converted to a morally sound position on the issue of slavery.

Before converting fellow Southerners, however, evangelical ministers first had to convince themselves of the goodness of slavery. They rejected as unbiblical the abolitionist position that the mere holding of slaves constituted a sin and separated the ownership of slaves from the undeniable abuses inflicted upon many of the slaves. They concluded that eventual emancipation had to be rooted in reforming the behavior of individual masters and in teaching the slaves how to be good, self-disciplined Christians worthy of being granted freedom.

John G. Jones was a Mississippian who had no moral qualms over slavery before he embraced Methodism in the 1820s and became a minister. After his conversion, he condemned slavery as "a great moral evil."[28] However, if Jones had publicly expressed such views in Mississippi after the abolitionist mailing campaign of the mid-1830s, he would have lost his ministry and most likely would have been forced to leave the state. Thus, he kept his critical stance on slavery to himself and preached a gospel of Christian stewardship to slaveowners. By the 1840s planters considered him so safe on the slavery issue that he was entrusted with Christian mission work among their slaves.

Jeremiah Jeter, a Baptist minister, followed a similar path in Virginia. Despite strong feelings against slavery and a vow never to become involved in the institution, he found himself in the possession of slaves after he married a woman who held slaves. Along with his wife, he was determined to be rid of this human property, but he found such a step to be utterly impractical. Virginia laws forbade the simple freeing of slaves, and provisions had to be made to remove from the state any slaves who were manumitted. Colonization of freed slaves in Liberia was out of the question because his slaves were opposed to being shipped to Africa and such a step, along with manumissions, would have broken up slave families whose members were owned by different masters. Jeter kept his slaves and soon felt much better about his role as a slaveowner when a pro-slavery pamphlet converted him not only to a scriptural defense of slavery but to the belief that slavery "may, under some circumstances, belong to the best order of society that human, or even divine, wisdom can devise."[29]

The Reverend Basil Manly, Jr., swayed by an antislavery tract he had read in 1847, told his father that he yearned for the "cessation of slavery for the south & negroes & for our selves" and prayed that God would make possible "a way of escape from it."[30] Within three years he joined his father, another slaveholding minister who had harbored doubts about slavery, in preaching a pro-slavery gospel. And so it went. Evangelical ministers suppressed their initial moral concerns over slavery by assuming the clerical responsibility of preaching the need for a moral relationship between the master and the slave in which benevolent stewardship would guide the enslaved toward Christian salvation.

The most noted Southern divine who harbored heartfelt reservations over slavery before beginning his career as a slaveholder and missionary among slaves was Charles Colcock Jones of Georgia. When exposed to abolitionist doctrines while a student at Princeton in the early 1830s, Jones found himself morally and spiritually conflicted. He wrote to Mary Jones, his cousin and future wife, that he was "undecided whether I ought to continue to *hold slaves*. As to the *principle* of slavery, it is *wrong!*"[31] Torn between all the ties that bound him to his plantation home in low-country Georgia and his very real doubts over the morality of slavery, Jones resolved his spiritual crisis by deciding to return home as a reforming missionary. He would devote his life to spreading the gospel among his and other slaves as an essential first step in preparing them for the responsibilities of freedom at some eventual, but never specified, time in the future.

Without a doubt Jones saw himself as a model Christian master who administered both to the material and spiritual needs of those, as he would put it, "people" whom God had placed under his care. And yet, as explicated in Erskine Clarke's study of Jones and of slavery in coastal Georgia, the good reverend was living a life of self-deception. His vague hopes for freeing his slaves receded ever further into the future and their religious instruction became ever more elusive. Despite his self-image as a kindly paternalist with the best interests of his slaves at heart, he reacted in 1857 as would any other slaveowner with rising debts when faced with recalcitrant slaves seemingly impervious to his will—he sold them. Long bothered by what he interpreted as the defiant behavior of Cassius and his wife, Phoebe, Jones decided to sell them when they ignored his requests for information on the whereabouts of their daughter Jane who had run away. To be sure, he stipulated that Cassius and Phoebe were to be sold along with their children as a family unit, and hence he realized a smaller profit than if the slaves had been sold separately, but he also ordered that they be sold to a planter in the upcountry, thus wrenching them away from the only kin and friends they had ever known. At a time when slave prices were escalating, the planter who purchased them not surprisingly soon sold them for a quick profit to a speculator in Savannah, who transported them to the slave markets in New Orleans, where the family was broken up and sold off to fill the labor demand for field hands on the cotton and sugar plantations of the Southwest. After the initial sale, Charles had written his wife, Mary, in a self-congratulatory tone that "conscience is better than money."[32] Phoebe and Cassius had no illusions regarding Charles's sense of self-righteousness. They well knew that they were being disciplined by Charles and converted into cash regardless of any consequences to themselves and their family. They put the record straight when they wrote a white trader that they had been sold "for spite."[33]

Unable to admit that he had become a hardened slaveholder, Jones denied the brutal, money-making reality of slavery and wrote tracts outlining a biblical defense of the institution. What was too painful to acknowledge in himself he projected onto the abolitionists and antislavery Republicans. The unlimited and morally corrupting power that he and other slaveholders wielded in forcing their slaves into submission was displaced onto the Republicans. At the outbreak of the Civil War, he denounced Lincoln's party for lacking even a "residuum of humanity and respect for the opinions of the civilized world[;] . . . Christianity with its enlightening and softening influences upon the human soul . . . finds no lodgment in the soul of that party, destitute of justice and mercy, without the fear of God, supremely selfish and arrogant, unscrupulous in its acts and measures, intensely malignant and vituperative, and persecuting the innocent even unto blood and utter destruction."[34] A slave might as well have been condemning his or her master.

Other clerics found in abolitionism a convenient scapegoat for explaining away their own inability or unwillingness to push for emancipation. Writing in 1840, the Virginia Presbyterian minister Robert Lewis Dabney all but thanked the abolitionists for the positive impact they exerted on Southern thinking regarding slavery. Were it not for their self-righteous meddling in Southern affairs, he reasoned, Virginia would have emancipated its slaves within the next twenty years. But as a result of the self-scrutiny the abolitionists forced on Southern whites, "we find emancipation more dangerous than we had before imagined. Who knows but that this uproar of the Abolitionists . . . may have been designed by Providence as a check upon our imprudent liberality." Sudden emancipation, he concluded, might well have resulted in "irreparable injury" to the slave.[35]

Evangelical propagandists for slavery undoubtedly soothed many Southern souls nagged by doubts over slavery. Upon reading in 1857 a defense of slavery by the noted Baptist minister Thornton Stringfellow, the planter William C. Preston urged a fellow South Carolinian to read the work as well: "It has wrought a change in my views which have been worrying me all my life."[36] However, there were limits to the evangelical support for slavery. Most ministers shrank from defending slavery as an unqualified positive good that should be perpetual. They still clung to their theological ideal of a South fully living up to Christian standards once evangelical tutelage had removed the sinful abuses of individual masters, converted the slaves, and thus prepared the ground for an eventual program of gradual emancipation. Although increasingly unwilling to go public with their views, an untold number of ministers continued to be troubled by slavery. In the privacy of his diary in December 1858, Benjamin Mosby Smith, a Presbyterian minister and professor in Farmville, Virginia, lamented: "Oh what trouble, running sore, constant pressing weight, perpetual wearing, dripping, is this patriarchal institution! What miserable folly for men to cling to it as something heaven-descended."[37]

Smith and other evangelical ministers were nearly unanimous in their opposition to two new positions staked out by the secular defenders of slavery in the 1850s. The first was polygenesis, the doctrine of pioneering racists such as Dr. Josiah Nott of Mobile that blacks constituted a distinct and permanently inferior race from whites. After the loss of four of his children to yellow fever in 1853, Nott became ever more obsessed with the belief that African Americans and their mulatto descendants were uniquely sickly and prone to spread such diseases as yellow fever. His *Types of Mankind*, published in 1854, expanded on his earlier essays in proclaiming the separate creation of the races in separate areas of the world. Nothing less than the biological survival of Southern whites required that they be separated, in effect quarantined, from the disease-ridden, inferior black race. Despite admitting to a British visitor that he detested slavery, Nott added that he saw the institution as the only way in which Southern whites could shield themselves from the presence of the blacks who would fatally contaminate them if ever freed.[38] Nott earned the contempt of the evangelicals for his dismissal of Christian paternalism for the slaves as a waste of time and his open rejection of the biblical teachings in Genesis that all humankind descended from the same set of parents. Nott might rant—"Just get the dam'd stupid crowd safely around Moses and the difficulty is at an end"—but the evangelicals were unmoved.[39]

The effort mounted in the late 1850s to reopen the African slave trade also elicited the nearly unified opposition of the evangelicals. Loudest in their denunciations were those evangelical ministers most closely identified with a slaveholding ethic of Christian paternalism for the slaves. For the Reverend James Henley Thornwell of South Carolina, the most renowned of the pro-slavery clerics who made the upholding of Christian ethics the centerpiece of his defense of slavery, the reopening of the trade would destroy what he called the *"humanizing element"* in slavery, the domestic and patriarchal feature of the institution in the South which ameleriorated the condition of the slaves. Inundated with dangerous and savage heathens from Africa, the South would have to resort to draconian police measures to ensure the safety of whites. World opinion would be shocked as the South morally regressed and endorsed what the Bible condemned as "manstealing."[40] John Adger, a fellow Presbyterian minister in South Carolina noted for his mission work in Africa and his call for spreading the gospel to slaves in the South, fully agreed with Thornwell and added that Southern participation in the trade would worsen tribal warfare in Africa and result in the separation of countless children from their parents.

The Fire-Eaters' Defense

Unlike the evangelicals, the states' rights fire-eaters were not bound by any limits, theological or otherwise, in their defense of slavery. Rather than enjoining slaveholders to fulfill their Christian responsibilities as masters or condemning the harshest, most dehumanizing features of the institution, the fire-eaters portrayed slavery as an absolute good. The crux of their appeal, both to themselves and other Southern whites, was just this insistence on the morality of slavery. They were uncomfortable with any moral ambiguities regarding slavery, including any queasiness over the African slave trade. "I regard the [African] slave trade as the test of its integrity," proclaimed Leonidas W. Spratt of South Carolina. "If that be right, then slavery is right, but not without."[41]

The push to reopen the African slave trade was centered in the South Carolina low country, a region in long-term economic decline.[42] Planters here hoped that an abundance of cheap African slaves would enable them to reclaim worn-out fields, reverse the displacement of slave labor in Charleston by immigrant Irish and Germans, and provide the South with the labor resources it needed to close the growing economic gap with the North without having to rely on white workers considered unreliable on the slavery question.

The movement's chief propagandists were young professionals on the margins of planter society. They preached their message with all the stridency of those recently converted to a great cause. Using as his pulpit the *Charleston Southern Standard*, a paper he purchased with the money from a financially advantageous marriage in 1851 that also left him as the manager of ten slaves, Spratt demanded that the South prove itself a civilization worthy of the name by removing the moral stigma placed on its origins by Congress when it prohibited the African slave trade in 1808 and then branded it as piracy in 1819. As his eloquence soared, he called on Southerners to grasp their destiny as a "chosen people" and demonstrate to their moral critics how "to work out the real regeneration of mankind."[43] The African slave trade, he insisted, was a providential agent of social and economic progress, and once the South recognized it as a moral good and reopened the trade, the rest of the world would be in awe of the greatness achieved by the slave South.

Henry Hughes, a young lawyer in Mississippi, was nearly as prominent as Spratt in the movement. As late as 1851, Hughes considered slavery to be morally wrong. As he wrote in his diary: "The relation of landlord & tenant is as sinful as that [of] master & slave. Both relations shall be abolished: but not to the hurt of the South."[44] Far from working to abolish slavery in order to soothe his conscience, Hughes fantasized slavery out of existence. His *Treatise on Sociology*, published in 1854, purported to find in the labor arrangements of the slave South, which he called "Warranteeism" rather than "Slavery," a blissful state of perfection that bordered on a utopia. The warrantor, that is, the slaveowner, saw to all the needs and wants of his laborers, who, in turn, provided faithful service. Thus, for Hughes, "The economic system in the United States South, is not slavery. IT IS WARRANTEEISM WITH THE ETHNICAL QUALIFICATION. It is just . . . The consummation of its progress, is the perfection of society."[45]

Hughes's defense of slavery earned him the public acclaim he craved and he soon found himself in the Mississippi Senate calling for the reopening of the African slave trade. When critics objected that a horde of recently arrived supposed savages from Africa would render hellish problems of slave discipline and endanger whites, Hughes responded with none of the comforting images of harmony that had suffused his depiction of the master-slave relationship in his *Treatise*. Instead, with an irony that probably escaped him, he proposed a barbarous system for identifying any imported Africans: "If necessary bloody letters may by State authority, be branded on the negroes' cheeks or chins." Should free-labor philanthropists recoil in horror at such a policy, then Hughes would contemptuously defy them: "let us if expedient to identify our new negroes, mark them like hogs and brand them like beeves; let us slit their nostrils; let us pinch in their bleeding ears, cross-cuts and underbits, or with hot and salted irons, fry on their brows and breasts, lasting letters ... Then let freedom shriek till her face is red, and her voice is cracked as her skull."[46] In his grotesquely savage rant, Hughes was lashing out against not only the abolitionists who tormented his conscience, but also the evangelical ministers in the South who viewed a revival of the trade as a repudiation of all their efforts to shape slavery according to Christian standards.

For all the attention they garnered, the slave traders gained surprisingly little political traction. Not a single Southern state legislature (South Carolina came the closest) endorsed their cause. At least as much a form of moral exhortation as a political movement with a realistic goal in mind, the movement called on Southern whites to reclaim their self-respect by casting aside all moral aspersions on slavery, including those on the African slave trade, in a bold defiance of world opinion. The slave traders had clearly moved beyond the mainstream of Southern white opinion, but the theme of self-respect at the core of their message exposed a raw nerve in the Southern white conscience that more skillful politicians could exploit with greater success.

William Lowndes Yancey of Alabama carved out a public career for himself in a melodious oratory that called upon Southern whites to regain their self-respect by throwing off the stigma of moral inferiority the Yankees had stamped upon them. He delivered one of his greatest performances at the Democratic national convention in Charleston in April 1860.

Yancey's traumatic childhood shaped an adult personality in which he acted out the psychosocial role of the aggrieved Southern white demanding from the North a recognition of the essential goodness of slave society.[47] Uprooted at the age of nine from his boyhood home in Georgia by his stepfather Nathan Beman, a stern Presbyterian minister who moved the family to Troy, New York, the adolescent Yancey stood by helplessly as Beman beat his mother and on more than one occasion locked her in a closet. Once back in his native North, Beman also took up the cause of abolitionism. For

Yancey, his abolitionist stepfather came to represent the North writ large—hypocritical, unbending, and cruelly self-righteous in its denunciation of slavery.

The Alabama fire-eater's speech at Charleston that triggered the walkout of Lower South delegates and split the Democratic Party into two hostile wings in the election of 1860 was an impassioned appeal to Southern pride. Just as Abraham Lincoln had done in his celebrated Illinois debates with Stephen A. Douglas, Yancey zeroed in on the morality of slavery as the core issue that had to be resolved. Turning Lincoln's logic on its head, he insisted that Northern actions based on the false premise that slavery was wrong had demoralized Southerners and sapped their will to stand up for their rights and equality in the Union. Only a direct, open acknowledgment of the moral soundness of slavery could purify the poisonous public opinion of the North, stop future aggressions against the institution, and steel Southerners for the defense of their rights and honor. To drive home his point, Yancey played on Southern fears that, as a result of outside meddling, slavery was now a ticking time bomb. "Ours is the property invaded—ours the interests at stake . . . You [Northerners] would make a great seething cauldron of passion and crime if you were able to consummate your measures. Bear with us, then, if, as we stand on what is but a sleeping volcano, we say to you, to you we will not yield our position."[48]

The Secession Frenzy and the Slaves' Revenge

Yancey's speech, and the subsequent rupturing of the national Democratic Party, set the tone and direction of the presidential campaign of 1860 in the cotton South. The Breckinridge Democrats ran a campaign based on emotion and fear, themes that resonated deeply as rumors of abolitionist-instigated slave uprisings swept across the South and a long, searing drought portended food shortages and hard times ahead. Tensions boiled over in a number of savage incidents as whites lashed out at increasingly restive slaves and even turned against themselves in a search for enemies to be destroyed.

On the morning of June 11 an enraged mob burned at the stake a slave accused of killing his master in Oglethorpe County, Georgia.[49] Two months later, and also near Augusta, a "negro boy" in the sheriff's custody on charges of killing a white man, was removed from his cell by a group of twelve men who gave bonds for his re-delivery. They took him out to a station on the Southwestern Railroad, conducted a kangaroo trial, and burnt him at the stake. They returned his ashes to the sheriff.[50] On August 2 in the South Carolina low country, a vigilance committee, "numbering 54 of the best men in the lower part of the District," drove off the family of Melvina Night for tampering with slaves. Before they did so, the vigilantes tore down the Nights' cabin and outbuildings and rained down twenty-five lashes on the bare back of the elderly mother, thirty-nine for each of her daughters, and "a number too great to be counted" for her son.[51] By the fall, vigilance committees were also policing slaveholders. One of them, Michael Buzzard of upcountry South Carolina, publicly chastised his neighbors for daring to mount a campaign demanding that he ship off to the West his troublesome slave Simon. He would not "be whipped into a pale of the slave by the proscriptive opinions, in the way of resolutions, which they have seen power to adopt."[52]

Not surprisingly, the drumbeat of reports of slave unrest was particularly frightening to white women living in the midst of slaves. After a year's residence on her husband's plantation on the Sea Islands of Georgia in the late 1830s, Fanny Kemble pointedly noted: "every Southern *woman* to whom I have spoken on the subject has admitted to me that they live in terror of their slaves."[53] Some women dealt with their terror by fantasizing a frightful retribution for those slaves whose defiant actions exposed their vulnerability. In the aftermath of John Brown's raid on the federal arsenal at Harpers Ferry in 1859, Amanda Edmonds of Loudoun County, Virginia, wished the worst for those local slaves accused of burning harvested wheat. "What ought to be done with them?" she asked in her diary. "I would see the fire kindled and those who did it singed and burnt until the last drop of blood was dried within them and every bone smolder to ashes."[54]

For Keziah Brevard, a wealthy widow who lived alone with twenty of her slaves at her residence near Columbia, South Carolina, the terror of what her slaves might do hung over her like a shroud during the fall of 1860 and on through the ensuing secession crisis. She had taken on much of the management of her deceased husband's plantations and had lived her life amidst slaves. Her experience had taught her that she knew nothing of slaves save that they lacked any moral sense, were aware of a lot more than they let on, and harbored a murderous rage to kill her. As her diary reported her sleepless nights and nightmares of fires raging out of control, she repeatedly referred to her dread of her slaves. She railed against the abolitionists for wanting Southern whites "murdered in cold blood because we own slaves" and made it clear that she felt most of her own and her neighbors' slaves would seize any opportunity "to butcher us." Like most Southern whites who expressed their views, she rejected any claims that slavery was a positive good. If she had had her way, she never would have owned slaves or chosen to live in a slave society. For her, slavery was an unsettling and endless source of anxiety, a burden she felt powerless to be rid of. Her one consolation was that she "never had a son to mix my blood with *negro* blood." As war approached in April 1861, she alternated her fear that at any moment "we may be hacked to death in the most cruel manner by our slaves" with the plaintive hope that God would "save us" and peacefully rid the South of its slaves by "send[ing] them away to a land they love better than ours."[55]

Offsetting this image of a tension-wracked society under siege so vividly depicted in Brevard's diary was the message of deliverance and social harmony presented by states' rights defenders of slavery. What ailed the South, they insisted, was not intrinsic to a slave society but the result of abolitionist interference with gullible slaves and the North's parasitic draining of the South's wealth through protective tariffs and control of the financing and marketing of its cash crops. Cut the Gordian knot of Northern attachment and the natural harmony of the South's slave-based society would assert itself and the South's agricultural wealth would make it the envy of all other nations.

South Carolina's John Townsend predicted in June that a Southern Confederacy would bask in "a prosperity, financial, commercial and manufacturing, which the South has never before enjoyed; and an abundant ability to defend herself against any aggressions, no matter from what quarter they may come." In this best of all possible worlds, slavery would be "established upon a basis of permanent security which it has never yet had," because Northerners would no longer feel any responsibility for the institution that they denounced "for its alleged sins and crimes." As for the possibility of secession touching off a war with the North, Townsend foresaw conflict only in the free states as labor and capital fought for their share of a collapsing Northern economy no longer propped up by Southern wealth. In a thinly veiled reference to a South Carolina economy seemingly in terminal decay, he boasted that any "signs of weariness and decrepitude" in the Southern economy unjustly attributed to slavery would vanish once an independent South freed itself of the Northern stranglehold. The South would then retain all that was its own and "[o]ur institution of slavery, too, will then redeem itself from the unpopularity and odium which has been cast upon it by the injustice of those who have robbed it of its rights."[56] This was the message pushed by hard-core secessionists throughout the 1850s, and the fact of Lincoln's election, a demonstration of Northern political power they eagerly anticipated and indeed welcomed, was all the incentive they needed to launch a campaign to convert the white masses to their revolutionary agenda.

South Carolina created the model of popular mobilization followed by the other states in the Lower South. The goal was to overcome the reluctance of those characterized by Townsend as the "apathetic disunionists," those who would have to be "lifted themselves over every mole-hill in the path" and the "Unionists *per se*," those who cunningly professed support for secession while scheming to patch together another self-defeating compromise with the North.[57]

He was confident the former were ripe for conversion if they were artfully led every step of the way; the latter might well need to be intimidated by the threat of force.

The South Carolina secessionists understood that poorly educated and semi-literate whites comprised the bulk of the audience they had to reach. Any effective appeal to them had to consist of more than the mass distribution of the secession pamphlets prepared by the 1860 Association, a propaganda organization funded by low country planters who shared Townsend's secessionist views. The secessionist appeal had to reach all the senses by combining the pageantry of a military parade, the speeches and hoopla of a political rally, the visual spectacle of a carnival, and the calls for salvation of a revival—all whipped into an intoxicating cocktail of seething emotions. The result was what whites across the cotton South routinely called the "great excitement," a feeling of being swept along in a grand collective experience that daily bombarded one's senses.

In the six weeks between Lincoln's election and the passage of South Carolina's ordinance of secession, public life in Charleston had all the earmarks of an endless street festival. Almost nightly, torch-lit processions marched through the streets to the accompaniment of fireworks, rockets, and the booming of cannons. With economic activity at a virtual halt once credit markets froze up in the political crisis produced by Lincoln's victory, businessmen and workers were a captive audience for one pro-secession speaker after another. They competed against each other in broadcasting their Southern loyalties by making secession banners and transparencies, erecting Liberty Poles, and wearing blue-cockades, knots of ribbons pinned to one's hat or clothing as an emblem of support for secession. Brightly colored and elaborately designed flags up to 24 by 26 feet in size provided symbols that tapped into a whole range of emotions mobilized in the push for secession—hatred of the abolitionists, mocking defiance of the Republicans, pride in the Southern heroes of the American Revolution, and the self-respect to be regained by leaving the Union. The flags also served as an unwritten text conveying scenes of the prosperity that awaited an independent South—

cotton bales stacked on wharfs; happy, contented slaves working in the fields; railroads carrying freight to the ports; and ships arriving directly from Europe with goods for the Southern market. Most of all, the flags and banners communicated the urgent need for immediate resistance against the threatening North.[58]

No other locale matched Charleston in the sheer frenzy of its secession mania, but the excitement was generalized across the Lower South. One form that it commonly took amounted to a purification rite in which a racially united community purged itself of the Yankee demon that was disturbing public order and peace. Soon after news of Lincoln's election reached Aiken, South Carolina, the citizenry turned out for a torch-light procession. The centerpiece of the procession was an effigy of Lincoln carried on a rail by two black men. When the procession halted, Lincoln's effigy was hung on a scaffold and set ablaze to the "cheers of the multitude."[59]

From his pulpit in New Orleans, Presbyterian minister Benjamin Palmer bestowed the most influential evangelical blessing on the secessionist cause in his Thanksgiving Day sermon of November 29, 1860. Starting from the premise that slavery was a "trust providentially committed to us," Palmer declared that secession offered Southern whites their only hope "of conserving and transmitting the system of slavery with the freest scope for its natural development and extension." This was the duty Southerners owed themselves, their slaves, the civilized world, and God himself. The only alternative was to submit to a Republican "reign of terror" led by atheistic, anarchistic abolitionists. As the truest and best friends of the black race, Southern whites understood that to free the slaves now or in the near future was to condemn them to extinction. The "most helpless" of all the races, they needed the caring protection of white masters for their very survival. Palmer contended that under the South's patriarchal system, the slave was "my brother and my friend: and I am to him a guardian and a father." Stripped of that protection and pitted into open competition against the superior white race, the freed slaves would "waste away through listlessness, filth and vice." Here, in this evangelical fantasy, was an imagined view of slavery that enabled Southern whites to cast aside moral qualms over the institution and transfer the burden of guilt onto their Northern tormentors. Palmer concluded his sermon by calling upon the South to grasp this "sublime" moment and accept the grace given it to "save herself, the country, and the world."[60] No wonder this soul-stirring oration in favor of secession was widely excerpted in the Southern press and run off in sixty thousand printed copies for distribution to secessionist groups.

The South Carolina secessionists were right: if their state took the lead, other slave states would follow. The momentum for secession generated in South Carolina proved to be irresistible across the Lower South. Driving it forward was the fear that to turn back now was to invite disaster. A surprisingly large number of whites reached the conclusion that the slaves believed that Lincoln's election heralded their emancipation. From her plantation in eastern North Carolina, Caroline Pettigrew reported that "I have not heard a dissenting voice to the fact, that the belief is prevalent among the negroes that this election decided their freedom—even small negroes have spoken as to their approaching freedom."[61] Faced with the "great annoyance" of slave runaways on the Savannah River in the winter of 1860–61, Charles Manigault concluded that slaves in many sections of the low country had "very generally got the idea of being emancipated when 'Lincon' comes in."[62] Fears of slave plots to strike for freedom spurred many of the worst excesses of the vigilance committees that sprang up before and after Lincoln's election wherever slaves were to be found.

How much this reflected the actual behavior and words of the slaves or a ratcheting up of jittery white nerves is unclear. What is clear is that Southern whites were never able to repress totally their anguish over holding slaves and that they grasped at some level that their slaves desperately wanted to be free. However much they sought refuge in the myth of benign paternalism or a pro-slavery reading of the Bible, the slightest disturbance to their social order brought to the surface what the editor of the *Newberry (S.C.) Rising Sun* called "the semi-devils of that black phantom."[63] His choice of words was revealing. Phantoms are illusory mental images, which in this case lodged in the white mind as the frightful revenge that the slaves would exact on the whites for all they had done to them under slavery. So deeply buried was their guilt that whites in the Lower South could imagine the black quest for freedom only in terms of a bloodbath directed against themselves.

Unlike whites in the Upper South who could accept, and in some cases promote, the gradual end of an institution they recognized as inherently wrong, whites in the plantation belts of the cotton South tried ever harder to convince themselves that slavery was right, indeed a providential blessing. Their rage over the refusal of the North to cease its moral condemnations climaxed with the election of Lincoln. Thus, the slaves did not have to engage in violent acts of rebellion to gain their revenge. They did so by daily giving the lie to the professed white image of them as loyal, docile servants content in their bondage, a lie frightfully revealed to whites when they sensed the first stirrings of the slaves' longing for freedom in the fall of 1860. Rather than facing up to that lie, and all that it implied of their moral character, whites in the cotton South found it less painful to embrace secession as the ultimate vindication of themselves and their slave-based society. As events were soon to show, and as silenced Southern conservatives had always predicted, secession was a suicidal, self-defeating rush to destruction.

ELIZABETH R. VARON

"Save in Defense of My Native State"

A New Look at Robert E. Lee's Decision to Join the Confederacy

"**SAVE IN DEFENSE OF** my native State, I never desire again to draw my sword." Robert E. Lee made this pledge repeatedly during the secession crisis, and it holds the key to understanding his decision to cast his lot with the fledgling Confederacy. Lee first articulated the vow in January 1861 in private letters to his children, siblings, and cousins, explaining to them why he resisted the Deep South's siren song of disunion. But as hopes for compromise faded, the "save in defense" formula took on new meanings for Lee and came to encapsulate why he felt he must join the Confederate cause. And so Lee repeated his vow, with some variation, in his April 20 letter to Winfield Scott tendering his resignation from the United States Army—and he invoked it again on April 23 as he accepted the command of Virginia's forces.[1]

There was nothing transparent or simple about Lee's pledge to defend Virginia. Rather it represented his complex effort to navigate the treacherous political crosscurrents of the era. Lee's pledge can be properly understood only when put in the context of Virginia's longstanding debates over disunion, of its distinctive political culture, and of its supercharged secession convention. His fateful decision in the spring of 1861 was a public drama. In the face of an active campaign by secessionists to recruit him to their cause, Lee, who was steeped in a tradition of pro-slavery Unionism, struggled to set the terms on which he would affiliate with the Confederacy.

In exploring his politics, this essay will offer an alternative to the prevailing image of Lee in the historiography. Remarkably, even as scholars have debated virtually every aspect of Lee's record and myth, a strong consensus has prevailed that his April 1861 decision was an instinctive, natural, and emotional act based on feeling and sentiment rather than ideological commitments or calculations. In choosing Virginia over the Union, Lee, we are told, followed his heart and not his head. In his enduring work of hagiography, *R. E. Lee: A Biography*, Douglas Southall Freeman describes Lee's embrace of the Confederacy as "the answer he was born to make." Lee did not even construe his decision as a "choice"—and once he had embraced the Confederate cause, he never looked back. On the opposite end of the biographers' spectrum is Lee's principal detractor, Alan Nolan, whose *Lee Considered: General Robert E. Lee and Civil War History* aims to knock Lee off his pedestal. Nolan rejects Freeman's view that Lee's identity as a Virginian predetermined his course of action. But Nolan, too, repeatedly attributes Lee's actions to his "feelings"— feelings of loyalty to the South and slavery and not simply to Virginia. In both interpretations, Lee is viewed as driven by emotion rather than political calculations.

In the middle of the spectrum of Lee scholarship are books that promise a dispassionate assessment of the "man behind the legend." For all their nuance and revisionism, these modern studies offer just so many variations on Freeman's "destiny" theory. According to Emory Thomas in his 1995 biography, although Lee cultivated a public detachment from politics, his views are simple to read: Lee's motives for secession "were exactly what he said they were." His loyalty to Virginia and the South "sprang from blood and bonds; in such a context the Union was a mere abstraction." Biographer Michael Fellman, ascribing to Lee a stoic passivity, asserts that he "followed the South into secession as a matter of second nature"—he chose the concrete loyalties to home and family and Virginia "against the far more abstract Union." Brian Holden Reid, for his part, argues that Lee embraced the Confederacy because he "had always preferred a world of hierarchy and deference," while the recent acclaimed study by Elizabeth Brown Pryor, *Reading the Man*, observes that Lee "made an emotional decision" and followed his "heart's truth."[2]

In fact Lee did not simply follow his heart. Rather, in the spring of 1861 he carefully transmuted his pro-slavery Unionism into a politically potent, though somber, rationale for secession. Lee's pledge was meant to extricate him ideologically from the terrible dilemma at the heart of Virginia's secession crisis.

Virginians Debate Secession

During the debates that unfolded over the secession winter of 1860–61, Virginians were faced with a choice between two deeply rooted philosophies of disunion. The older of the two philosophies cast disunion as fundamentally evil—as a tragic outcome of political extremism—and posited that if civil war came, it would utterly destroy Southern society and the institution of slavery. The other, insurgent, philosophy cast disunion as a positive good and posited that if civil war came, the slave South would triumph and prosper.

Each position had its own complex genealogy. When Virginia Unionists warned in the state's secession convention that disunion was a "deep, dark vortex" that would destroy the South, they tapped a longstanding association in Southern politics of disunion with extremism and anarchy. By 1861 Southerners had already, for half a century, used images of national ruin to cast a protective spell over slavery. Leading antebellum politicians such as Andrew Jackson and Henry Clay stigmatized abolitionists as disunionists; these Southerners imagined disunion as a sort of mutually assured destruction and insisted that to desire it was fundamentally irrational and functionally treasonous. In debates over the extension of slavery into the Western territories, slaveholders repeatedly conjured disunion as a race war and a brothers' war and asked, in effect, "Who in their right mind could want that?"[3]

But on the political margins, disunion was redefined. In the 1830s, militant defenders of slavery, alarmed by the rapid rise of abolitionism, pledged themselves to "disarm disunion of its terrors"—to imagine it, for Southerners, not as a fearful calamity, but as the prelude to the successful establishment of an independent Confederacy. This states' rights vanguard, led by Robert Barnwell Rhett and James Henry Hammond of South Carolina and Edmund Ruffin and Nathaniel Beverley Tucker of Virginia, insisted that the Union was a revocable compact, a treaty of sorts, between the states; that the central government was subordinate to the states; and that state sovereignty legitimated secession as a mechanism of protest and self-defense. They resorted to emotionally charged disunion rhetoric to drum up resistance to immediate abolitionism. Thus Arthur Trevor, the principal protagonist in Tucker's fire-eating 1836 novel, *The Partisan Leader*, rejects the traditional view that disunion was the "maximum of evil" and comes to believe instead that the antislavery North itself was the source of all evil and that disunion was preferable to "subjugation." It was just such a conversion that the states' rights vanguard hoped to effect in the Southern electorate.[4]

Over the course of the 1840s and 1850s, Southern moderates assiduously resisted the efforts of the aspiring secessionists to "disarm disunion of its terrors." Apostles of Clay, such as Virginia's stalwart Whig John Minor Botts, defended the political middle ground by stigmatizing the secessionist fire-eaters as fanatics who shared the abolitionists' dark and irrational wish to push the country to the brink. And it was not only Southern Whigs of the nationalist pro-compromise school who disparaged disunion. Deep into the antebellum period, Southern Democrats too, when it seemed politically opportune, invoked disunion as an accusation—albeit one leveled exclusively at antislavery Northerners. For example, when Northerners protested the Fugitive Slave Act in the early 1850s, none other than the leader of the fire-eaters, Robert Barnwell Rhett, warned that Northern defiance of the federal government would "crush beneath it . . . all faith, brotherhood, and peace, until the whole fabric [of the Union] falls a vast pile of ruin and desolation."[5]

Such accusations of Northern disunionism rested on two premises: that the antislavery political parties could be stigmatized as just so many vehicles for Garrisonian extremism, and that a shared loathing of the abolitionists could sustain the fragile intersectional alliance between pro-slavery Northern and Southern Democrats. And for a very long time, well into the 1850s, the accusations worked: they served both to marginalize antislavery forces as extremist and to define pro-slavery Unionism as the conservative, mainstream position in the slavery debates.

It is little wonder, then, that when Virginia's Unionists sought to rally their followers in the winter of 1861, they tapped time-tested images of disunion as mutually assured destruction. In its initial stage, the Virginia secession convention, which met for the first time on February 13, was dominated by a coalition of Douglas Democrats and John Bell Whigs. Most of these men were conditional Unionists whose continued fealty to the federal government was predicated on Abraham Lincoln's repudiating coercion of the seceded states. Some, concentrated in the state's northwestern counties, were unconditional Unionists. As historian William Link explains, for them "coercion" was not a key issue; rather, these delegates were pledged to uphold the Union no matter what. The Virginia coalition was held together by the conviction that disunion would destroy the South. Drawing graphic pictures of the horrors of civil war, Unionists argued that when war came, it would be a "carnival of death," as delegate George Brent of Alexandria memorably put it. It is little wonder, too, that these Unionists inveighed against the reckless radicalism, the "folly and wickedness," of both Northern abolitionists and Deep South secessionists. As John Minor Botts intoned, "South Carolina is a very extreme State—Massachusetts is another . . . I do not think it just to take either as reflecting fairly the conservative sentiment of either section of the country."[6]

Virginia's Unionists, both conditional and unconditional, bolstered their case with an elaborate argument about their state's exceptionalism—about its special geographic and historic role as a bulwark against sectional extremism. Virginia was positioned, they argued, at the center of the Union; with her mixed economy, she shared the material interests of both North and South. If the South seceded, they warned, Virginia would be perched on the border of the new

Confederacy and would be especially vulnerable to the "ravages of civil war" and to slave rebellion and flight. She would be consigned to "stand guard and play patrol for King Cotton." Unionists also invoked the "centripetal influence of [Virginia's] moral power," as delegate Waitman T. Willey put it: Virginia alone, as the "principal architect" of the Union, had the authority to act as mediator in the nation's great hour of peril. This was a recurring theme among the convention's leading Unionists. "It is hers to be faithful when all others shall prove faithless; it is her duty, when all others shall forget duty, to stand by it to the last," the venerable George W. Summers intoned; the "ancient Virginia school," John B. Baldwin added, was the "school of compromise."[7]

The secessionists, for their part, more determined than ever to disarm disunion of its terrors, made emotionally resonant counterarguments, ones that they had been busy perfecting since the late 1850s. The Republicans' strong showing in the 1856 election had signaled the disintegration of the anti-abolition front, as the Northern electorate gravitated toward the free-soil movement. Consequently, the Southern rights vanguard drew the conclusion that the Democratic Party could no longer be relied upon to protect slavery—and they stepped up their campaign to convince the Southern electorate that disunion, under the right conditions, need not be dangerous or uncertain at all. In their region's newspapers, colleges, churches, commercial conventions, literature, and other public forums, secessionists built the case that if the South were divided, weak, and uncertain, Republicans would prosecute a war that brought all the horrors Americans had long associated with disunion—a war of chaos and massacre, a descent into the abyss. But if the South were united and strong, it could quickly and decisively turn back any Northern invasion and build, in the form of a new nation, an impenetrable bulwark against future aggression.[8]

To promote Southern unity, secessionists imputed to the leading Republicans not a crippling irrationality but rather a design for dominance. In the eyes of the fire-eaters, Lincoln's "House Divided" and William Seward's "irrepressible conflict" speeches of 1858 seemed to signal that the North had given up on compromise and was ready to impose its will on the South. John Brown's failed 1859 attempt to liberate Virginia's slaves was widely interpreted in the white South as the fruit of the intemperate rhetoric of leading Republican politicians. The Republicans' nefarious plan, so the secessionists claimed, was to start a war of conquest in which emancipation would be imposed at bayonet point.[9]

The most important theme in the secessionists' bid for regional unity was the bright prospects of a putative Southern Confederacy. Yes, there was an "irrepressible conflict," Virginian Roger A. Pryor declared in 1859, but a united South would emerge the victor: an abolitionist army of "conscience-stricken traitors" was no match for "eight million Southern freemen, educated to the use of arms." Those freemen were ready, Pryor promised, to "rear a government which shall survive the lapse of ages."[10]

In Virginia's convention, secessionist delegates portrayed their Unionist foes as just so many stooges of the abolitionists. To Unionist suggestions that Virginia essay another peace proposal, secessionists responded that it was degrading for her to go "cap in hand, through the weary round of supplication." To Unionist suggestions that Virginia shared economic interests with the North, secessionists responded that the Old Dominion could fully develop her economic resources only if removed from the rapacious competition of Northern industries. To the Unionists' claim that the commonwealth's historic role was that of mediator, secessionists countered that the "Virginia[ns] of 1776" had not been "chilled with fear" but had instead moved vigorously to defend their rights. As Robert Montague put it, "Virginia was the first State on this Continent that ever exercised the great doctrine of secession," when she severed her connection with Great Britain. And to the Unionist case that disunion would be a "carnival of death" in which the institution of slavery itself would be destroyed, secessionists countered that the South had all the advantages in the coming conflict and that the greatest advantage of all was slavery itself. Montague noted with pride that "Virginia was the great pioneer of the institution"and thus it was fitting that she should lead the way in its defense.[11]

The most damning sin of the "Black Republicans," these men agreed, was that they had repudiated and slandered the luminaries of Virginia's glorious past: Washington and Jefferson, Madison and Monroe. As George Richardson put it, in a key speech in early April 1861, "Abolitionism, that fiendish libeller, says *cursed be they for they were slaveholders.*" No true Virginian could let the slander go unanswered. No true Virginia *man*, that is. Secessionists delighted in portraying Unionists as weak and effeminate. The "lamenting" and "weeping" of Unionists was nothing short of "nauseating," ex-governor and ardent secessionist Henry A. Wise declared in early April. His message to them: "you ought to enter the lists like men."[12]

Secessionists, in short, manipulated the language of disunion and the notion of Virginia's distinctiveness in order to convert citizens of "conservative sentiment," and particularly the conditional Unionists who dominated the convention, to their radical cause. "The question of Union or Disunion is dead and buried," declared an article in the *Staunton Vindicator* in March 1861. Virginia faced a stark choice, the writer explained, between joining her "sister States" or "subordination of [her] section to Black Republican and abolition aggression and outrage." Secessionists promised to those white Southerners who joined the cause, among many other bounties, political and moral clarity—an end to the long, harrowing debates over the causes and imagined consequences of disunion and a new emphasis on martial vindication.[13]

Robert E. Lee's Secession Crisis

This brings us full circle back to Robert E. Lee. His letters to his relatives during the secession winter, in which he describes his struggle to choose sides, echo the language of the era's leading Unionist politicians—from national figures such as Henry Clay to local leaders like Botts—in his linking of secession to anarchy and revolution.

For example, in January 1861, Lee lamented to his son Rooney: "I can anticipate no greater calamity for the country than a dissolution of the Union. It would be an accumulation of all the evils we complain of . . . Secession is nothing but revolution." Well into the winter of 1860–61, Lee's letters about secession were dark and despairing. It seemed to him that "kind Providence" had "turned the current" of God's blessings away from Americans. He bemoaned the fact that his countrymen had shunned the legacy of the founders, who had, in Lee's view, designed the Union to be perpetual. And as so many leading Unionists did during the state's convention, Lee also lamented that Virginia seemed to be turning away from her ancient role as mediator; he noted that when disgruntled New Englanders had proposed secession at the Hartford Convention of 1814, it had been Virginians who stood firm against this heresy.[14]

Most of all, Lee decried the Deep South fire-eaters' imperious rhetoric and militant demands, such as the reopening of the slave trade. "I am not pleased with the course of the 'Cotton States,'" he confided to his son Custis in December 1860. "Their selfish, dictatorial bearing . . . argues little for the benefit or peace of Va. should she determine to coalesce with them. While I wish to do what is right, I am unwilling to do what is wrong, either at the bidding of the South or the North." Lee was keenly aware of the secessionists' litany of grievances but showed little interest, as he made his painful choice, in conjuring the dire consequences of Republican rule.[15]

Nor, for that matter, did Lee conjure slaveholders' glorious prospects in the Confederacy. In three letters he wrote at Fort Mason, Texas, in late January 1861, to his first cousin Martha Custis ("Markie") and to his sons Custis and Rooney, Lee introduced his "save in defense" pledge coupled with a prophecy that the coming war would be a "fiery ordeal" for his beloved Virginia. To Markie he professed his profound love of the Union, "a government inaugurated by the blood & wisdom of our patriot fathers, that has given us peace & prosperity at home, power & security abroad, & under which we have acquired a colossal strength unequalled in the history of mankind." If this Union were torn asunder, he pledged he would "go back in sorrow to my people & share the misery of my native state, & save in her defense there will be one soldier less in the world than there is now." To his sons he repeated this promise to "share the miseries" of his people and to again draw his sword for Virginia's defense alone.[16]

Lee clung to the narratives of "disunion as evil" and "Virginia as mediator" so late into the secession crisis because they accorded with the Federalist/Whig tradition of his family and, paradoxically, with Lee's soldier's ethos, which demanded that professional warriors, officers especially, shun demagoguery and privilege nation over faction. He subscribed to a Madisonian understanding of the nature of the Union, one in which, as political scientist Rogan Kersh has explained, "affective connections among the people were required to secure political bonds between the states" and in which "affective sentiment, not a unity imposed by the central state, was the soundest basis for a common national life." As late as the last days of January 1861, as he undertook his journey back from military duty in Texas, which had recently seceded, to Washington, D.C., to report to General Winfield Scott, Lee held secessionists responsible for attenuating those affective bonds. He insisted that the secession crisis was brought on by "folly" and "selfishness," and that disunion would be a "fearful calamity."[17]

Leaving the Union

Three months later, Lee was a Confederate. So how did he, in the end, "disarm disunion of its terrors?" Lee's decision to resign was on one level a deeply personal one, a drama that played out, in its last crucial act, in the confines of the Lee-Custis mansion at Arlington, where Lee agonized, in isolation, before informing his kin of the verdict on the morning of April 20. But Lee's agonizing was also a public drama. In order to make sense of his decision, we must recognize that Virginia's own secessionists cannily recruited him into their ranks, tailoring their theory of Virginia's distinctive role as the progenitor of the American Revolution to Lee's own family history.

Rumors about what course Lee would choose began to circulate in the Virginia press in February 1861, as the state's secession convention commenced its deliberations. The *Richmond Dispatch*, for example, noted that "Virginia has sons in the U.S. Army who, in the event of her invasion, would, beyond all doubt, assist in her defense . . . Such men as Col. Robert Lee, who has no superior as a soldier in the United States, ought to be placed at the head of her forces." The *Alexandria Gazette* opined: "We do not know, and have no right to speak for or anticipate the course of Colonel Robert E. Lee . . . But if he should resign his present position in the Army of the United States, we call the immediate attention of our State to him, as an able, brave, experienced officer . . . His reputation, his acknowledged ability, his chivalric character, his probity, honor and—may we add, to his eternal praise—his Christian life and conduct—make his very name a 'tower of strength.' It is a name surrounded by revolutionary and patriotic association and reminiscences." Secessionists in effect promised that Lee's ascendancy into the elite ranks of the new Confederacy would restore the luster of the Lee name (wiping clean the blot of his father Lighthorse Harry's fall from grace). And they argued that, given his lineage, the mantle of revolutionary would fit more comfortably on Lee's shoulders than the mantle of mediator.[18]

For a time, Lee seemed immune to such appeals. Well into April 1861, Lee, at home in Arlington and following the news through the Alexandria newspapers, continued to resist the idea that secession was Virginia's destiny and his own. Then came the turning point. Lee, like so many of his fellow Virginians, was jolted out of his indecision by Lincoln's April 15 call, in the wake of the Confederate firing on Fort Sumter, for troops to suppress the rebellion. The "last feather which breaks the camel's back has been applied," explained the formerly Unionist *Lynchburg Virginian*—Lincoln had at last revealed his determination to invade the South. Upper South Unionists, who had clung to "seemingly authoritative reports" that the Lincoln administration "intended to pursue a peace policy," felt that they had been betrayed. On April 17, the Virginia convention—now meeting in secret session—passed a secession resolution by a margin of 88 to 55; a similar resolution had failed to pass twelve days earlier. A critical number of conditional Unionists, who had been awaiting proof of Lincoln's willingness to use coercion, had moved into the secessionist column.[19]

Even as it severed Virginia's ties to the Union, the convention strategized about how best to secure Lee's services. On the heels of the vote for secession, delegate Jubal Early recommended that the convention consider Lee as a candidate for command of the state's military forces. Early was a conservative Whig from Franklin County who had deprecated secession in much the same language as Lee himself—he even voted with the "nays" on April 17—only to side with Virginia when the deed was done. On the following day, Early was seconded in recommending Lee by Henry A. Wise, who had long called for military resistance to the Lincoln administration.[20]

Lee's crisis now entered its acute stage. Lincoln's call to arms in effect demanded of Lee that he do the unthinkable: "raise my hand against my relatives, my children, my home," as he put it.[21] Lee's wife, Mary Custis, in a letter on his decision, expressed their shared belief that the Union was now an "empty name," its flag "dishonoured" by the Republicans. To make matters worse, on April 18 Lee—as yet unaware of Virginia's secession vote or the convention's interest in him—was summoned by Lincoln's intermediary, Francis Preston Blair, and offered command of the Union's army of coercion. Lee declined the command, telling Blair that while he regarded secession as "anarchy," he could *not* consult his "feelings in this matter" and must follow the dictates of duty instead. Lee then promptly sought out his mentor, Winfield Scott, general-in-chief of the U.S. Army, for an interview. Lee consulted that day with his brother Sydney and cousin Cassius Lee, too. But they could not restore his lost confidence in the Union and in the political process.[22]

Lee learned of the Virginia convention's vote on the morning of April 19. But even then he could not bring himself to accept the "positive good" school of disunion thought; "I must say that I am one of those dull creatures that cannot see the good of secession," he confided to a fellow Alexandrian that day. What was Lee to do? That night he agonized, pacing the floor at Arlington, as his family waited in suspense. By midnight he had come to his decision.[23]

At this crucial juncture, Lee again invoked his pledge. In three letters that he wrote on April 20—to Winfield Scott, tendering his resignation from the army, and to his sister Anne Marshall and brother Sydney Lee, explaining that decision—Lee repeated the vow that save in defense of Virginia, he would not draw his sword. In these letters, the pledge no longer signified Lee's dread at the prospect of disunion; it was no longer coupled with references to Lee's sharing the "misery" of his people. Now the pledge signaled Lee's belief that Lincoln's April 15 call for troops and the attendant secession vote of the Virginia convention, on April 17, had snapped the affective bonds that had sustained the Union. Lee had hoped, he wrote his brother, to wait until Virginia's citizens had ratified the convention vote before making his own decision. But once Lincoln called for a military force to suppress the rebellion, war was, as Lee saw it, a reality. The scenario he had envisioned with regret during the secession winter—that a Union built on "brotherly love and kindness" was to give way to one that could "only be maintained by swords and bayonets"—had materialized.[24]

Lee tailored the pledge to the recipient of each letter. For Scott, it came in the context of Lee's expressions of gratitude to the general for his "uniform kindness and consideration." To his sister Anne in Baltimore, an unconditional Unionist, Lee confessed that he recognized "no necessity" for secession and would have "pleaded to the end for redress of grievances, real or supposed." He inserted into the pledge a new clause, meant to enlist her sympathies: "save in defense of my native State, with the sincere hope that my poor services may never be needed, I hope I may never be called on to draw my sword." And to Sydney Smith Lee, a U.S. Navy commander who would soon accept a commission in the Confederate Navy, Lee wrote of his duty as a soldier not to remain in the U.S. Army when he was "liable at any time" to be given orders that he "could not conscientiously perform."[25]

In these evocations of his pledge, Lee reimagined disunion, not as the Unionists' descent into the abyss or the secessionists' ascent to glory, but rather as a solemn act of state allegiance. This state allegiance was not, as Freeman and subsequent Lee biographers would have it, a simple expression of blood and bonds, of instinct and emotion. Indeed, in his wife Mary's view, Lee "relinquished . . . the security of his home & family" (as the federal occupation of Arlington would dramatize) in fealty to his greater duty: namely "*to defend* his state." To further complicate the notion that Lee simply followed his heart in rendering his decision, his daughter's account said of Lee that "the army had been his home and his life" and that only his "sense of duty" made him leave it.[26]

State allegiance was for Lee—a man who had spent most of his adult life away from Virginia in service to the U.S. Army—every bit as much a political abstraction as the Union itself. Lee's fealty to the Old Dominion rested on nostalgia, peculiar to Virginia's political culture, for the days of the early republic when the other states "almost took it for granted that Virginia would be their leader." It rested on an ethos of self-preservation that had justified Virginia founders such as Jefferson in their defense of slavery as a "necessary evil"— a system that could not be dismantled without endangering the state's security. And it rested on a historical consciousness—an awareness that long, long before there was a Union, there was Virginia, a veritable "country" of its own. None of these ideas was incompatible with American nationalism, and none was synonymous with states' rights doctrine. Indeed Lee's nostalgia was for the great age of nationalism embodied by Washington, Madison, and his own fervently Federalist father, Harry Lee. But all of the ideas encouraged Virginians to imagine that the state had the first claim on their loyalties—a claim that stretched back to the seventeenth century. John Janney of Loudoun County, the staunchly Unionist president of the Virginia convention, declared in explaining his own willingness to abide by the convention's final secession vote, "I am, in a word, a Virginian—a citizen of a Commonwealth that had existed as a sovereign organized government for two hundred years before the United States had a name." If Virginia lost its primacy in the Union, the Union was no longer sound. If their ancient mother called them back, men like Lee reasoned, they must heed the call.²⁷

Lee, who revered George Washington, was surely aware that in his last will and testament, Washington had bequeathed his sword to his nephews with the injunction that they should never draw the sword except in "self-defense or in the defense of the Country and its rights."²⁸ With the Union a shambles, Lee concluded, the time for self-defense was at hand. In rendering his decision, Lee insisted that Virginia's duty was neither to mediate the conflict nor lead the revolution, but instead to protect her own moral and territorial integrity.

Joining the Confederacy

On April 19, the Virginia secession convention resolved to contact Lee. On April 20, after he had resigned from the U.S. Army, Lee got word that the authorities in Richmond wanted to meet with him. The following day he received a summons from Governor John Letcher of Virginia, himself a Douglas Democrat who had moved into the secessionist column late in the game, after Lincoln's call for troops. On April 22, Lee undertook the journey by train to Richmond. News of his impending arrival had gotten out, and he was cheered along the train route by well wishers and met at the station by an enthusiastic crowd. Lee was escorted by a delegation of local leaders to his hotel and on to his meeting at the capitol with Letcher, where he accepted command of the military and naval forces of Virginia.²⁹

From April 20 through the evening of the 22nd, speculation was rife within the convention as to Lee's whereabouts and his political disposition. On the 20th, delegate Lewis Harvie, an early proponent of secession who had long since lost his patience with the skeptics, suggested that if Lee (and Joseph E. Johnston, who was the convention's second choice for commander) failed to come forward promptly, the delegates should invite the president of the Confederate States, Jefferson Davis, to "take charge of the military operations of the state of Virginia." Two days later, with Lee's intentions still unclear, Harvie suggested a second time that Virginia give over its militia to the Confederacy. Harvie wanted to know: was Lee coming or not?[30]

At this juncture, delegate William Macfarland of Richmond jumped in to defend Lee—and to buy him time. Macfarland, another Whig conditional Unionist who had just entered the secessionist ranks, informed the committee on April 22 that Lee had indeed resigned his commission in the U.S. Army and that he was at that very moment en route to Richmond. Harvie retorted that while he did not mean to cast an imputation against Lee, neither could he see any good reason for the convention to delay: the passage of Virginia's ordinance of secession "was invitation enough to all her sons in the service of the United States to rally to her standard." The absence of a military leader on the scene in Richmond had led, Harvie complained, to a "state of perfect disorder." He added, "such a condition of things should not be permitted to exist for one day."[31]

Macfarland again took up Lee's part, insisting that his arrival was imminent and that no military decisions should be made before his appearance. To wait for Lee was to show him, Macfarland reminded the delegates, "a very becoming respect." The delegates should not be surprised that Lee had not yet revealed his intentions; he was a military man who could accept no offer until it was made through official channels.[32]

Later that evening, the convention finally received for its approval Governor Letcher's formal nomination of Lee for the position of major general in command of Virginia's military and naval forces. Early felt vindicated. "Whether we have the right of secession or revolution," Early declared, hedging his bets on the constitutional issues at stake, "I want to see my State triumphant." "I do believe that it will be triumphant under the lead of Major-General Lee," he told the convention. Early was joined in paying homage to Lee by another former Unionist, John Critcher, who expressed his pride that both Lee and Washington hailed from his own Westmoreland County. Harvie, for his part, supported Lee's nomination, but only after noting one last time that "if General Lee had failed to come forward," he for one would have felt "no cause of shame in fighting under the banner of Jeff. Davis." Harvie's secessionist colleague, delegate Leonard S. Hall of Wetzel County, asked for reassurance that Lee's appointment would not "trammel us in any action we may take towards a union with the Confederate States." He received such assurance from Janney.[33]

From the start of the convention, secessionists such as Wise, Hall, and Harvie had outdone Unionists at mobilizing popular support in Richmond; an endless round of torch-light processions, stump speeches, and "spontaneous" Southern rights meetings had animated the streets of the city. The evening of April 22 was no different. A pro-secession crowd, along with the First Regiment Band, stopped first at the Exchange Hotel, to serenade Confederate vice president Alexander H. Stephens, who was in Richmond to secure Virginia's entrance into the Confederacy. The Georgian obliged the crowd with a short speech about how Virginia's sister states in the South were blazing with Confederate fervor. The crowd then proceeded to the Spotswood House to serenade Lee, whose appointment was a secret no longer. Lee, who disliked crowds, declined to appear; the mayor of Richmond, Joseph Mayo, paid Lee's respects, by proxy, to the serenaders.[34]

The process culminating in Lee's nomination serves as a reminder that Virginia's decision for secession was in fact a series of decisions. Having voted to submit its secession ordinance to Virginia's electorate for ratification on May 23, the convention in the meantime had had to set up a provisional government and system for the state's defense, and at the same time had to decide on the terms under which that provisional government and army would affiliate with the Confederacy. While the events of April 15 through 17 (Lincoln's call for troops and the convention vote) had resigned Lee—along with Letcher, Janney, Early, Critcher, Macfarland, and many other "reluctant rebels"—to secession, those events had not dispelled the tensions and antagonisms within the convention. It remained for Virginians to decide what sort of army they would field, and what kind of war they would fight.

Once the convention had unanimously confirmed Lee as major

general, it set about orchestrating a formal ceremony to dramatize the significance of his appointment. At Macfarland's suggestion, the convention voted to receive Lee at noon on April 23 into the Hall of the House of Delegates—this was a fitting tribute, he noted, as "a similar ceremony was observed upon the appointment of the immortal Washington." The "moral influence" of such a ceremony for Lee would "remain in the hearts and the memory of the entire country." Macfarland's proposal sparked a warm exchange over whether the convention would remain in secret session or receive Lee in the open. It settled on a proposal to meet behind closed doors to keep out the crowds—but to insure that it made the very most of the moment, the convention agreed to invite the governor and his council and the Confederate vice president Alexander Stephens to witness Lee's investiture. Delegate James W. Sheffey of Smythe County, a longstanding secessionist, suggested that the convention should stand as it received Lee.[35]

Every delegate was on his feet on April 23 when Robert E. Lee entered the Hall of the House of Delegates in the state capitol on the arm of delegate Marmaduke Johnson, another Unionist recently converted to secession. The president of the convention, John Janney, presided. The past month had been a prolonged nightmare for him. He had watched secessionists like Wise, a man whose "overweening influence" Janney deplored, seize momentum in the convention by invoking the defense of Southern honor and manhood against the threat of Northern radicalism and coercion. A northern Virginian, Janney had a strong ideological affinity with Lee; indeed Janney's letters to his wife as the convention unfolded were eerily similar, in their tone of disbelief, to Lee's missives to his own relatives. Just six days earlier, on the day of the secession vote, Janney had disparaged disunion as the ultimate horror—a civil war, he forecast presciently, would make northern Virginia a Flanders field, with the Potomac as its Rhine, "saturated with human blood." "I desire to know of gentlemen here today if any power that ever governed any civilized nation upon the face of the earth, ever plunged their country into a war with such fearful odds against them," Janney pointedly asked his colleagues. He thought the answer to be "no"—but out of loyalty to his state, Janney had stayed on as convention president, to aid the commonwealth in preparations for its self-defense. He would soon return to northern Virginia and retire from public life.[36]

On this day, April 23, Janney welcomed Robert E. Lee with a stirring speech that alluded to Lee's noble lineage and to the Revolutionary War record of his "gallant father." Janney suggested that Lee now take up the mantle of none other than George Washington, and he carefully noted that Washington's warrior ethos accorded perfectly with Lee's: "when the Father of his Country made his last will and testament," Janney declared, "he gave his swords to his nephews with an injunction that they should never be drawn, from their scabbards, except in self defense, or in defense of the rights and liberties of their country." Janney trusted, he said in conclusion, that Lee would draw his sword only in Virginia's defense. Lee, in his short response to the convention, one last time repeated his pledge: "I devote myself to the services of my native State, in whose behalf alone, will I ever again draw my sword."[37]

The omissions in this exchange were conspicuous. Neither Janney nor Lee mentioned the Confederacy, its grievances against the Yankees, or its glorious prospects. At this moment more than any other, Lee's pledge had multiple meanings. It was clearly a rebuke to the Republicans, and more broadly to the antislavery North, for having broken faith with Southern moderates and particularly with patriotic Virginians like Janney and Lee. At the same time, Lee's renewed vow—that for Virginia *alone* would he draw his sword—doubled as a rebuke to the Deep South extremists and to their Virginia acolytes, for their intemperate demands, predictions, accusations, and hatreds.

Although it seemed his day of triumph, Lee did not get the last word. The Confederate vice president Alexander Stephens now took the stage and delivered a long, strident speech that reprised many of the themes of his famous "Cornerstone" address, delivered in Savannah a month earlier. Stephens himself had been a latecomer to secession; once he had seen the light, he assumed the role of vice president precisely to represent the eclipse of Southern Unionism and to woo the hesitant to the cause. This he did with stirring invocations of the superiority of the new Southern government over the now repudiated Union. While the old Union rested on the misapprehension that slavery was evil, the new Confederacy's cornerstone, Stephens asserted in Richmond as he had in Savannah, was the "inferiority of the African."[38]

Stephens at this moment did not merely echo his earlier address. He retooled it to fit the new circumstances. In March, speaking to Deep South secessionists who nervously watched the proceedings in the Upper South, Stephens had offered predictions and reassurances: the "border sister slave States" such as Virginia, would, he predicted, "assimilate" with the principles of the Deep South and join the Confederacy. But even if they did not, he reassured his listeners, the Confederacy, resplendent in resources and righteousness, would still thrive and succeed. Now in late April, Stephens indulged in a cool piece of revisionism, telling the Virginia convention that he had always regarded the state's secession as "inevitable." Appealing to the delegates' state pride, he noted that the Confederacy was committed to defending the constitutional principles that were the "great work of Virginia statesmen"—principles that Northerners had recklessly betrayed.[39]

Stephens's goal was to steel Virginia's convention into taking the next step: to join the Confederacy and to place the state's resources in the hands of the new nation. And so, on April 23, alongside his appeals to the native pride of the delegates, he delivered what amounted to a rebuke to Janney, Lee, and all of those Virginians who had over the winter and spring of 1861 made the Confederacy wait and wait. Such indecision was no longer tolerable, with the "enemy now on your border," he warned. Virginia would not and could not stand alone, Stephens explained, but must instead immediately put herself and her military "under the direction of the Confederate States Government." Stephens noted that personally he had held out against secession and accepted it only once Georgia's convention had delivered its verdict. He had quickly come to see that Georgia's interests were synonymous with the Confederacy's. "So I trust it will be in Virginia," he intoned. "Your cause is ours, your future will be ours," he told the delegates, and "your destiny must be ours." Stephens's speech proved to be prophetic. In May, Virginia formally joined the Confederacy and in June its troops came under Confederate control. Lee's state commission as commander-in-chief proved nominal, superseded by his appointment as general by the Confederate Congress in June 1861.[40]

Even as Lee relinquished his hope that Virginia might somehow chart her own moderate course, his pledge worked, inexorably, to bind the new Confederacy together. Virginia's secession convention had moved quickly, on April 23, to arrange the "immediate publication" of Lee's speech accepting his state commission. "Nothing would be more pleasing to our constituents," delegate Macfarland predicted. He, too, proved prophetic. In Virginia and throughout the South, Lee's long-anticipated appointment as Virginia's commander-in-chief "made a sensation." When Lee "pledged himself" to perform "his whole duty to the land of his birth," the *Richmond Dispatch* reported, he had a "magic influence on the citizens" of the commonwealth. Indeed the press in Virginia held Lee up as the model citizen: "Virginia expects every son of hers," the *Lynchburg Virginian* declared, in an article on Lee's decision, to "do his duty now" and "act like Lee." Deep South secessionists, for their part, rejoiced that Virginia could at last offer the Confederacy a standard bearer. Confederate newspapers as far south as Macon, New Orleans, and Dallas crowed that the South now claimed the "first soldier of the age." "With such men to the fore," the perceptive Confederate diarist Mary Chesnut put it, "we have hope."[41]

These commentators understood that Lee's decision not only had profound military implications for the South, but profound political implications as well. For in extricating himself from the secession dilemma, Lee had also extricated his fellow Southern moderates. Here was the lasting legacy of Lee's pledge. His emphasis on self-defense and state allegiance as the essence of the "Cause" sent an unmistakable and enduring message to white Southerners: namely that they need not subscribe to the secessionists' radical political agenda in order to feel duty bound to the South.

The war itself would radicalize Lee and make of him a committed Southern nationalist. The North's willingness to shed blood and to target noncombatants, the courage and sacrifices of the Southern volunteers, the federal occupation of his Arlington estate—these trials of war gave credence to the very secessionist arguments that Lee had once rejected. State allegiance for Lee became synonymous with states' rights, and Virginia's interests synonymous with the South's. Over the course of the war, Lee would come to embody for the Confederate public the very essence of Southern nationalism.[42] But not before one last season of doubt, during which Lee's detractors wondered where his true loyalties lay.

In May and June 1861, Lee threw himself into mobilizing Virginia troops and preparing them for war. Nonetheless, a few of those close to Jefferson Davis doubted that Lee's heart was in it. For example, Davis confidante Albert Taylor Bledsoe wrote to the Confederate president that Lee did "not know how good and how righteous our cause is and consequently lacks the one quality the times demand." Lee's sober prophecies that the war would be long and hard, Bledsoe reckoned, were "calculated to dispirit our people." Questions about Lee's loyalty occasionally flared up in public, in the press. Some Northern papers speculated that Lee regretted his decision to resign from the U.S. Army, and that he was "shedding bitter tears" at his mistake. Southern newspapers countered such rumors. One Georgia paper reported in mid-July 1861 that Lee was "heart and soul in the cause, working in every possible way to strengthen the condition of the South, and render her triumph complete." But rumors proved persistent and were fueled by Lee's performance in the field. His first major combat assignment—to subdue insurgent Unionist counties in western Virginia—ended in failure, with the Confederate defeat at Cheat Mountain in September 1861. Among the many reasons for the setback was Lee's inability to coordinate the efforts of his subordinates, Generals Henry A. Wise and John B. Floyd (both former governors of Virginia). The Richmond newspapers the *Enquirer* and the *Examiner* (to which Wise and Floyd had close ties) called Lee "Granny Lee," an epithet that alluded to his ripe old age of 54 and to his associations with "Granny Scott," as the Confederate press had dubbed Lee's former mentor Winfield Scott. The epithet also echoed the secessionist accusation that Unionists lacked manly courage and resolve. In another gendered aspersion, *Examiner* editor Edward Pollard charged that Lee's "extreme tenderness of blood" had prevented him from taking the fight to the enemy.[43]

Lee was depressed by this criticism but not deterred by it. He waited for his chance at redemption, and it came during the Seven Days Battles in the summer of 1862. Lee's brilliant generalship in his defense of Richmond against George B. McClellan began his apotheosis as the preeminent symbol of the South. From that point on, Confederates could tell the story they had longed to tell: that once Lee had pledged himself to the Cause, there was "no questioning, no holding back, no delay."[44]

During the war and after, Lee's hagiographers, from Early to Freeman, would wash the politics, and with it much of the drama, out of Lee's secession crisis.[45] But something critical is lacking in such a "Lost Cause" view of the origins of the war. We cannot forget, as we try to explain what propelled "reluctant rebels" into the Confederate ranks, what had held them back in the first place. For Lee's secession crisis dramatizes the observation made by military historian Russell Weigley that "always there was a psychological rift deep inside Southern purposes." Southerners had been "nurtured from birth in the civic religion of United States nationalism." They could not "shake off their nurturing so abruptly as secession and the creation of the Confederacy demanded." That rift, one that Confederate ideology was not able fully to close, derived, it might be said, from deep ambivalence about disunion itself. White Southerners had been nurtured in the use of disunion as a dark accusation—defenders of slavery had for decades hurled curses at the abolitionists for conspiring to undo the republic. If it was not so easy to shake off the old faith in the Union, neither was it easy for white Southerners to shed their fear that disunion, so long dreaded, would bring in its wake a long train of tragedies.[46]

On April 23, 1865, four years to the day after the Virginia convention bestowed on Lee command of the commonwealth's army, Lee granted an interview to a reporter from the *New York Herald*. Naturally the reporter was eager to obtain Lee's first-hand account of the recent surrender at Appomattox, and Lee obliged. But the reporter was just as interested in Lee's fateful actions in April 1861 as he was in the verdict of April 1865. Referring specifically to Lee's pledge—to his "determination to draw his sword in defense only of his native state"— the reporter asked what "degree of deliberation he had given to that expression." In his answer, Lee at first hewed to the orthodoxy of Southern nationalism. He had been, he assured the reporter, a "firm and honest believer in the doctrine of States Rights." But as Lee continued, the nature of his political commitments, and of his 1861 pledge, came more clearly into view. In explaining how he construed states' rights, Lee avoided any mention of constitutional theory and instead proposed that "his allegiance [was] due primarily to the State in which he was born and had always resided." When Lee "accepted service under the rebel government,"recorded the journalist, "he did so on the principle that he was defending his native State." It was his duty "to abide by [Virginia's] fortune."[47]

Had this creed of state allegiance and self-defense, in the end, worked? Had it disarmed disunion of its terrors? The answer is probably no—Lee's Southern nationalism could never entirely displace his sense that disunion had turned the current of God's blessings away from Americans. "He opposed secession to the last, foreseeing the ruin it was sure to entail"—this is the impression Lee left on the *New York Herald* reporter who interviewed him on April 23, 1865.[48] Although he had embraced the principles of Southern nationalism, Lee was vindicated, tragically, in the one tenet of his Unionism that he never gave up: his belief that the war would be fierce, long, bloody, and destructive. Lee's decision reminds us that some of the reluctant rebels of his generation knew all too well what disunion would bring.

ROBERT J. COOK

The Shadow of the Past

Collective Memory and the Coming
of the American Civil War

THE SHADOW OF THE past fell heavily on Americans before the Civil War. Notwithstanding their reputation for pragmatism, present-mindedness, and forward-thinking, they worried frequently about their relationship to yesteryear. In the fraught early decades of the nineteenth century, fears abounded that the first post-independence generation might not be up to the task of preserving the legacy of republican government bestowed by the Founding Fathers. Even the country's solid (if far-from-stellar) military performance in the War of 1812 failed to dispel gnawing doubts about the sustainability of the founders' nation-building achievements. Against a rising tide of intersectional tension over slavery and slavery expansion, some Americans, especially those of a moderate or conservative political disposition, regarded attention to history as an essential tool for strengthening national bonds. One of the most celebrated of all the Founding Fathers, James Madison, lived into ripe old age. During the 1820s he prepared his notes on the secret debates at the 1787 Philadelphia convention for posthumous publication, intending them to serve as an indispensable historical guide to wise action in the future. When South Carolina nullifiers threatened to sever their state's connections to the Union over the tariff issue, Madison made public his conviction that his own Virginia Resolution of 1798 had been merely declaratory and that it had, in any event, never been intended to assert the right of an individual state to invalidate federal legislation.¹

By the late antebellum period there were signs that filiopietism was in something of a decline at all levels of the polity. Young Virginians, for example, blamed their elders for what they justifiably regarded as their state's waning political influence in the counsels of the nation. They favored economic diversification to halt declension and, somewhat paradoxically, a more vigorous defense of slavery against Yankee assaults. Growing numbers of Southerners and Northerners, moreover, were beginning to sense that the founders' compromises over slavery would not hold. James Madison's responses to the divisions occasioned by slavery extension—colonization of blacks, diffusion of slaves across geographical space, and reliance on historical precedent—seemed wholly inadequate to the seriousness of the situation, not least because (as Madison himself discovered during the nullification crisis) there was no sign of a consensus over what the lessons of history might be.²

Yet retaining for the most part their respect for the achievements of the Fathers, mid-nineteenth-century American politicians continued to reference the remote and recent past in their appeals to the voters—to embarrass their opponents, to impart greater conviction to their arguments, and to fashion themselves as legitimate heirs of patriotic statesmen. In October 1854 Stephen Douglas and Abraham Lincoln locked horns in Peoria, Illinois, to debate the controversial Kansas-Nebraska Act. Douglas, the Democratic senator who had introduced the territorial bill, attacked his Whig opponent for betraying the nationalist legacy of Henry Clay and Daniel Webster on the grounds that he (Lincoln) rejected popular sovereignty as the optimal compromise solution to the slavery extension controversy. In a powerful three-hour speech, Lincoln denied the charge and, seeking certainty in an increasingly contested American past, depicted popular sovereignty as antithetical to the Revolution's central principle of self-government. "The spirit of seventy-six and the spirit of Nebraska, are utter antagonisms;" he warned, "and the former is being rapidly displaced by the latter."³

The onset of the secession crisis indicated no let-up in the politicians' desire to win popular support by appealing to their personal interpretations of history. Every day during those confused winter months Northerners and Southerners drew on vast stores of inherited knowledge to try and make sense of the events going on around them. This essay probes the function of collective memory in the coming of the Civil War. While scholars have observed the commitment of Northerners and Southerners to their particular interpretations of the Revolution, they have done little to assess how politicized uses of history influenced Southern secession, the failure of compromise, and the outbreak of war at Fort Sumter. Emotionally powerful, regionally segmented memories of a recent past freighted with grievances eventually took precedence over those fraternal "mystic chords" of Patriot memory that U.S. president Abraham Lincoln, on William H. Seward's advice, summoned on behalf of peace in his first inaugural address. This was no accident. As the sectional conflict entered its deadliest phase, politicians on both sides of the Mason-Dixon line battled to persuade ordinary Americans that they and not their enemies were on the right side of history.

Modern scholarship on the construction of human memory highlights the inherently political nature of what we know to be a complex process. Memory is part of the fabric of human identity, essential to who we are or at least who we think we are. Unless or until somebody invents time travel it is not possible to relive the past as it actually happened. The past may not literally be a foreign country as the English novelist L. P. Hartley wrote famously in *The Go-Between*, but it is certainly gone for good. Individuals remember it imperfectly and in many different ways. In a critical insight the French sociologist Maurice Halbwachs, a pioneering influence on modern memory studies, contended "that a person remembers only by situating himself within the viewpoint of one of several groups and one or several currents of collective thought."[4]

Put another way, remembering the past is most usefully seen as a process of social construction. Individuals in the modern era recall the past by looking at photographs, talking to friends and family, browsing the Internet, listening to the radio, reading books and newspapers, and watching movies and television. Together with the inexorable passage of time and the dictates of human self-interest, these mediating agents help to ensure that two people can "remember" the same event in very different ways. The same holds true of people acting collectively. Modern nation-states generate national memories, grand historical narratives of a country's past that are constructed wittingly by powerful individuals and groups with a stake in crafting a particular and (they hope) broadly unifying interpretation of their country's history. Normally these "official" memories do not go uncontested. Minorities often develop potent "counter-memories" which, for the most part, are ignored or marginalized by groups with greater access to state power. During the 1850s, for example, free people of color and their Northern white allies fashioned a distinctive narrative of the American Revolution that emphasized the positive role that black men had played in landmark events like the Boston Massacre and the Battle of Bunker Hill. Although this alternative account was at odds with the lilywhite nationalist "memory" of the Revolution, it revealed the capacity of collective narratives to influence action in the present. Northern free blacks used it to promote their claims for equal rights and to demonstrate what they saw as their quintessentially American commitment to freedom in the escalating conflict with the disloyal pro-slavery South.[5]

Swirling memories of all kinds influenced the way individuals and groups reacted during the secession crisis, impelling them not only to draw what they took to be meaningful parallels between the past and the present but also to act upon those putative lessons of history. When President Abraham Lincoln asked his cabinet for counsel upon learning in early March 1861 that the federal garrison at Fort Sumter was fast running out of supplies, he received conflicting opinions, several of them grounded in their respective author's understanding of past historical events. Simon Cameron, secretary of war, opposed reinforcement on the grounds that it would require the dispatch of "at least 20,000 men" and render the harbor "a Sebastopol"—a highly charged allusion to the protracted fifteen-and-a-half-month Allied siege of the imposing Russian fortress in the Crimea that had gripped the western world in 1854–55. Attorney General Edward Bates, like Cameron a former Whig, premised his argument for withdrawal on the impending threat of "servile war," bloody slave insurrection in a destabilized South. Although he did not make the allusion specifically, Bates was conjuring memories of fear-inducing slave insurgencies like that of the Haitian Revolution of 1791–1804 and Nat Turner's 1831 rebellion in Southampton County, Virginia. The only cabinet member who recommended reinforcement at this stage was Montgomery Blair, a Republican of Democratic lineage whose father, Francis Preston Blair, had been a fiercely nationalist member of Andrew Jackson's cabinet at the time of the nullification crisis. "It is obvious," noted Postmaster General Blair, "that rebellion was checked in 1833 by the promptitude of the President in taking measures which made it manifest that it could not be attempted with impunity and that it [rebellion] has grown to its present formidable proportions only because similar measures were not taken."[6]

It would be easy to deduce from this evidence that while memory may have influenced individual opinion during the secession crisis, it had little impact on how the crisis actually played out. In this instance arguments based on individuals' reading of the past failed to deliver a consensual verdict on which the new president could act. There is nothing surprising about this. Individuals often make what they believe to be reasoned judgments based on their reading of the past and come up with widely differing ideas about how they or others should behave in the present in light of those judgments. Lincoln's cabinet officers interpreted the past as it was refracted through their education, reading preferences, personal experiences, family ties, partisan allegiances, and political ideology. Viewed in isolation like this, individual memories appear to lack cohesion and, therefore, significant agency. In fact, personal memories *were* important during the winter of 1860–61 for the simple reason that certain individuals, none more so than Lincoln himself, possessed more power to influence events than others. This is particularly true in the case of the evolving Fort Sumter crisis. But importantly, *pace* Halbwachs, the memories of individuals were themselves socially conditioned. Politicians on both sides of the Mason-Dixon line were heavily influenced by, and were aware of, potent collective memories that assumed the status of grand historical narratives. These narratives possessed the capacity to exercise a controlling force on the behavior of all Americans during the secession winter.

We But Tread in the Path of Our Fathers

Antebellum Americans, not only native-born whites but also European immigrants and many Northern free blacks, lived their lives in the shadow of one dominant event, the American Revolution—one of two major historical reference points for political debate during the secession crisis. Even though most Revolutionary War veterans were dead by the spring of 1861, the legendary deeds of the Minute Men at Concord and Lexington, the winter suffering of Washington's Continental Army at Valley Forge, and the heroics of Patriot soldiers at Saratoga and Yorktown exercised a strong pull on all Americans during the first six decades of the nineteenth century. Like all memories, Revolutionary War memory was immensely malleable. (It remains so today, as evidenced by the attempts of modern-day Tea Party activists to employ it in the service of their conservative political agenda.) Its primary function, however, was a nationalizing one. From the late eighteenth century onwards, Revolutionary War veterans, school teachers, gentlemen historians, partisan newspaper editors, and professional politicians used the country's treasured moment of genesis to teach a national morality tale. The United States, all young Americans learned, was conceived in war as a missionary republic committed to liberty and opposed to tyranny. One of the main tasks of all parties during the winter of 1860–61 was to marry their own versions of history (as well as their particular visions of the future) with this founding narrative, which underpinned bi-sectional support for the Union during the first half of the nineteenth century. To do this they had to create alternative, or at least revised, narratives in order to persuade large numbers of Americans that their policies would build on the world-historic achievements of the Revolution's citizen-soldiers and esteemed founders like Washington and Jefferson.[7]

Radical states' rights secessionists had the hardest task in this respect because they were actively seeking to break up the United States, precious fruit of the Revolution in which Southern and Northern Patriots had suffered, fought, and died. Notwithstanding the heightened ire that debates over slavery and slavery expansion caused on both sides of the Mason-Dixon line from the time of the Missouri crisis onwards, a majority of white Southerners remained emotionally attached to the Union in late 1860. This was the reason why, even before Lincoln's election, hardline pro-secession newspapers sought to cut the affective ties that still bound most Southern whites to the United States, primarily by insisting that the Union of the Fathers no longer existed. "Many may remember and love it [the Union]," contended Robert B. Rhett's *Charleston Mercury*, "as it was in past days of usefulness and glory, when it was the Union of the Constitution. But now,—as it is *now without* the Constitution—*with* its furious sectionalism, and its anti-slavery fanaticism and policy at the North—the only feelings in the South which it can rationally inspire, are those of distrust, fear, contempt or hate."[8]

These efforts to shake Southerners from their avowedly delusional nationalism increased apace once the Republican victory was announced. The fiercest intra-state debate over the wisdom of secession occurred in Georgia. Here Thomas R. R. Cobb, a talented slaveholding lawyer, publicly revoked his unthinking attachment to the Union in a hard-hitting speech to the state legislature, quickly disseminated as a pamphlet, on November 12. "I bade selfishness avaunt, when my heart turned toward the Government of my fathers," he confessed melodramatically (but with manifest purpose). "I saw the glories of Bunker Hill, and Monmouth, and Saratoga, and Yorktown, clustering around it.—I recalled the story of her struggles as an aged ancestor who bled in her cause recounted it to infant ears around the winter's fire. I remembered a father's instructions, and had witnessed a father's devotion, and I fell down and worshipped at a shrine where he worshipped before me, and dared not to inquire into the cause of my devotion. But when the cruel hand of northern aggression aroused me from my worship, when it tore away the thin veil which covered the idol before me, I could but weep as the heartstrings were snapped from their attachment, though I woke to discover that I had been bowing before a veiled prophet of Mokannah, whose deformity and ugliness disgusted while they pained me."[9]

Georgia's many opponents of immediate separate-state secession (so-called Cooperationists) were appalled by what they regarded as foolish and manipulative attempts to break the ties of nationhood. Benjamin H. Hill sought to counter insurrectionary rhetoric by invoking the kind of historical memories that Cobb was trying to blot out. "Some men are honest, wise, and prudent," he told his fellow legislators pointedly, "[o]thers are equally honest and intelligent, but rash and impetuous." Lauding "[o]ur glorious revolution," Hill urged Georgians to act calmly like George Washington, the father of his country, at Fort Necessity in the French and Indian War, rather than rashly like the hot-blooded British general Edward Braddock who had perished in the same action. Alexander H. Stephens, a conservative Whig whose reading of classical history convinced him that ambitious demagogues constituted the main threat to ever-vulnerable republican polities, had no doubt that rabble-rousing fire-eaters were attempting to seize local power by appealing to the worst "passions and prejudices" of the masses. "Their object," he confided, was "to hide the truth" by exaggerating the threat posed by a Republican administration. "Had revolution been forced upon us as it was upon the colonies by a violation of principle," he mused, "by the assertion of unjust power incompatible with our security and safety, my hopes and views of the future would be altogether different from what they are." On November 14, the wizened Stephens tried to persuade the Georgia state legislature that Lincoln would be powerless without a Republican majority: "He will be in the condition of George the Third (the embodiment of Toryism), who had to ask the

Whigs to appoint his ministers, and was compelled to receive a cabinet utterly opposed to his views." The efforts of both Stephens and Hill to mobilize history in the service of caution were in vain. Subjected to intense pressure by secessionists and the drift of events, the two men ultimately sided with the Confederacy. Union sympathizers in the Upper South, however, had more political space to champion a romantic view of the nation rooted in Americans' common struggle for liberty in the eighteenth century.[10]

Senator Andrew Johnson of Tennessee delivered a strong pro-Union speech in Congress in mid-December. He was not, he said, "willing to walk out of the Union growing out of the Constitution, that was formed by the patriots and, I may say, the soldiers of the Revolution." Added Johnson, whose power base lay in the mountainous eastern portion of his state, "When we look around in the four States of Tennessee, Kentucky, Virginia, and Maryland, there are things about which our memories, our attachments, and our associations linger with pride and with pleasure. Go down into the Old Dominion; there is the place where, in 1781, Cornwallis surrendered his sword to the immortal Washington." In the Virginia secession convention, Unionists deployed a battery of arguments against secession, including the contention that secession would result in the future ruin of the state. But it was the Revolutionary past that Morgantown lawyer Waitman T. Willey evoked in a last desperate attempt to avert secession in April 1861. Among his constituents, he said, was his "old, patriotic father, born amid the thunders of the Revolution." "My son," the ancient had told him, "save this Union, or never let my eyes rest upon you again."[11]

Although impatient secessionists often contested these sentimental appeals to Patriot memory by pouring scorn upon them, most recognized the need to engage intellectually with their opponents' claim that deranged radicals were attempting to destroy a strong, prosperous Union won by the blood sacrifices of the founding generation. Their central riposte was that secession was the only practical way to guarantee the future security of the South's slave-based society against the accelerating attacks of Northern abolitionists. One line of argument, therefore, was to follow Chief Justice Roger B. Taney's reasoning in the *Dred Scott* decision of 1857. They pointed out to wavering Southerners that Republicans would pervert the racially exclusive intentions of the founders. The ultra Thomas Cobb was at pains to tell the Georgia legislature that the Republicans' alleged defense of slave-stealing and black suffrage slandered "[t]he memory of our fathers." It was a view echoed by Mississippi's secession commissioner to Georgia the following month. "Our fathers made this a government for the white man," intoned William L. Harris, "rejecting the negro, as an ignorant, inferior, barbarian race, incapable of self-government."[12]

Most Confederate leaders (relatively moderate pro-slavery men in the main) acknowledged the traction of Revolutionary memory and looked to position the Confederacy as the direct heir of the founding generation. In adopting this approach they were in some respects assisted by the fact that the Declaration of Independence was, in the words of one modern historian, "the first formal secession proclamation in world history." Thus did Jefferson Davis say on taking leave of his fellow Mississippians en route to Montgomery to accept the presidency of the Confederacy, that "we but tread in the path of our fathers when we proclaim our independence, and take the hazard." He made the same point in his inaugural address on February 18 when he stated that the new nation highlighted "the American idea that governments rest upon the consent of the governed, and that it is the right of the people to alter or abolish governments whenever they become destructive of the ends for which they were established." Many scholars have noted the derivative nature of early Confederate institutions and symbols. President Davis failed to get his wish that the Stars and Stripes should be adopted as the flag of his new nation, but the plundering of the federal Constitution and the placing of George Washington on the seal of the Confederacy made the point that Southern independence was grounded firmly and legitimately in the Revolutionary past. In this way the South's conservative leaders could direct their people toward a new future outside of the corrupted United States without threatening to destabilize the existing social order in which their own power was rooted.[13]

The Revolution was no less a focal point for Northerners during the secession crisis than it was for Southern whites. In the lead-up to the 1860 presidential election, Republicans had striven hard to counter Democratic claims that they were disunionists. On the contrary, Abraham Lincoln had argued in his February address at Cooper Union in New York that the Republicans were the true conservatives. Their signature policy of opposing the extension of slavery, he claimed, was entirely consistent with the founders' long-term objective of placing slavery on the road to extinction. The Republican candidate himself was an autodidact steeped in the kind of Revolutionary lore that Southern Unionists like Johnson and Willey were prone to invoke. His youthful imagination had been fired like that of many antebellum Americans by reading Mason Locke Weems's popular *Life of George Washington*. On February 21, 1861, President-elect Lincoln told the New Jersey state senate that Washington's exploits before and during the crucial Battle of Trenton had made a lasting impression upon him: "The crossing of the river; the contest with the Hessians; the great hardships endured at that time, all fixed themselves on my memory more than any single revolutionary event . . . I recollect thinking then, boy even though I was, that there must have been something more than common that those men struggled for."[14]

Lincoln's intention at Trenton was to underline his central point that he regarded the Union and the principle of popular government that underpinned it as perpetual. When Republicans invoked Revolutionary War memory during the secession crisis, they normally did so to make the case for confronting the secessionists with force.

James Watson Webb, a staunchly nationalistic Whig-Republican who edited the *Morning Courier and New-York Enquirer*, was one of the shrillest Northern advocates of coercion. He was mocked as "Chevalier Webb" by his Democratic rival James Gordon Bennett of the *New York Herald* for his apparent thirst for war. On January 8, 1861, Webb outlined his essentially historical argument for suppressing "those who have plotted Treason." Alluding to his middle-class readers' familiarity with the fate of Greek and Roman republics, Webb began by acknowledging that "'[t]he horrors of civil war,' are made familiar to every student of history," but added that these were "the greatest curse that can befall any people, save only the anarchy which civil war is designed to prevent." Modern governments, he insisted, were "the legitimate fruits" of "six thousand years of experiment and experience." The greatest of them all, in terms of its influence on others, was that of the United States. Its seeds were planted in America during the colonial era by "God in His Providence," then nurtured during the Revolution by "our fathers" who were tested by God in "a seven years' struggle with the mightiest nation of the earth; and in the school of adversity and suffering." The result was the American republic, *"the Union of these States*—intended to secure to our fathers, to us, and to our descendants forever, the blessings of Civil and Religious Liberty, and to become not only an asylum, but a beacon light to the oppressed of the Old World, teaching by our example, the ability of man for self-government." Modern Northern Patriots, Webb insisted, must confront the "Traitors and Rebels" now raising "their hands against the great work of our fathers" if the fruits of the Revolution were to be transmitted "unimpaired to posterity, even at the cost of civil war the duration of which no man can calculate."[15]

Although it is difficult to judge popular attitudes during the secession crisis with any degree of precision, there can be no doubt that the historical memory of the Revolution exercised a profound grip on ordinary Northerners and was intrinsically linked to their strong (though by no means unanimous) commitment to an unbreakable Union. One New Yorker was moved to write to Senator Andrew Johnson after the Tennessean's "magnificent and patriotic speech" in December 1860. Gushed the anonymous citizen, "As the descendant of one whose sword and fortune were devoted to the Revolution, to the creation of this noble fabric, which mad men & fanatics, are now shaking to its centre, I thank you." Keen to stiffen Abraham Lincoln's backbone over Fort Sumter, another New Yorker,

Mary Hancock Colyer, sent the new president an autograph of her uncle, the Boston merchant John Hancock, who had been a leading figure in the independence struggle. Colyer told Lincoln that she "humbly" trusted "it may prove an happy augury of our country[']s future history 'The Cradle of Liberty—' 're-built' by John Hancock and Abraham Lincoln."[16]

The Revolution's capacious memory lode, however, was as pliable as any other such trove. During the winter crisis it was mined not only by secessionists and stiff-backed Republicans but also by Northern conservatives who proved particularly adept at deploying it to promote their goal of a durable sectional peace treaty. The *Troy Daily Whig*, which had supported Constitutional Unionist John Bell for president, insisted that any attempt to coerce the seceding states back into the Union would repeat the mistake of the arrogant British during the War of Independence. "When the Colonies revolted," argued the *Whig*'s editor, "the argument in England was, this handful of rebels must be put down, and with all our power, we shall make short work with them.—This pride of power has been digging the graves of tyrants and swallowing up governments ever since the world was made ... [L]et us ... assert by all proper means that ours is the Government of the Old Union—the Government founded by WASHINGTON."[17]

Yet it was not only the Republicans' Northern opponents who tried to make America's Revolutionary past serve the cause of compromise. The former New York Whig William Seward operated at the heart of the new Lincoln administration. He was distrusted by many leading Republicans, not least Francis Preston Blair, a feisty Jacksonian warrior who considered him a schemer in the mold of the corrupt eighteenth-century British premier Robert Walpole. In fact Seward was not a proponent of peace at any price. His efforts to stave off civil war by preventing the secession of Virginia and the other Upper South states grew out of his attachment to the Union as a fraternal endeavor as well as a belief that "[n]ext to Disunion itself, I regard civil war as the most disastrous and deplorable of national calamities, and as the most uncertain and fearful of remedies for political disorders." Intriguingly, he compared his actions to those of one of the leading personalities of the War of Independence—not an indigenous Patriot hero as one might expect but William Pitt, First Earl of Chatham. The former British prime minister had tried to prevent war between Britain and its seditious colonists in the early 1770s but had ended up siding with the government's coercion policy. Knowing the importance of Revolutionary War memories to border-state and Upper South Unionists, Seward seized the chance to put those memories to good use when Lincoln invited him in late February 1861 to comment on a draft of the inaugural address. He moved to make the relatively uncompromising speech more palatable to the South's many conditional Unionists not only by revising or striking out certain phrases but also by adding a new peroration invoking the spirit of the Revolution.[18]

Increasingly persuaded by the New Yorker's conciliation strategy (at least insofar as it was designed to prevent a potentially disastrous second wave of secession), Lincoln rewrote Seward's workmanlike prose into the most lyrical passage of any presidential address. "I am loth to close," he ended the speech. "We are not enemies, but friends. We must not be enemies. Though passion may have strained, it must not break our bonds of affection. The mystic chords of memory, streching [sic] from every battle-field, and patriot grave, to every living heart and hearthstone, all over this broad land, will yet swell the chorus of the Union, when again touched, as surely they will be, by the better angels of our nature." Crucially, however, the new president did not, in the course of his inaugural, betray the majority of his co-partisans who regarded the struggles of the American Revolution as one very good reason to get tough with Southern rebels. The nation's perpetuity, Lincoln maintained unflinchingly, was "confirmed by the history of the Union."[19]

The War against Slavery

That history, of course, encompassed much more than sentimental tales of Patriot derring-do in the Revolution. Republicans and secessionists hostile to compromise turned to more recent sources of collective memory to construct political narratives that would render redundant most or all talk of settlement with the enemy. These narratives encompassed the sectional confrontations of the previous thirty to forty years and were characterized less by dewy-eyed romanticism than a stony, unforgiving sense of grievance on both sides of the burgeoning North-South divide.

Secessionists took a dim view of the various compromise efforts underway in Washington during late 1860 and early 1861. These efforts jeopardized their Southern independence project by fostering delay and uncertainty: compromise would relegate the radicals to the margins of power once again, enabling pro-slavery Unionists to frustrate their aims as they had done throughout the 1850s. One of the secessionists' main weapons against compromise was a coherent and internally consistent account of American political history since 1830. Although the precise details differed, the central message of the narrative was the same. For at least three decades, went the story, Northerners, jealous of Southern wealth and power, had been seeking to attack slavery. They did so first in the guise of the early abolitionist movement, then through congressional efforts to deprive Southerners of their constitutional right to take slaves into the common territories of the Union, and more recently in Republican-sponsored efforts to obstruct enforcement of the Fugitive Slave Act and to undermine the security of slavery in the states. Thomas Cobb told the Georgia legislature on November 12 that in order to expose the danger posed by "the triumph of Black Republicanism . . . it becomes necessary for us to go back a little in history." He proceeded to reference abolitionist petitions for the abolition of slavery, Northern politicians' efforts to repeal the Gag Rule (which had prevented discussion of those petitions in Congress), attacks on the domestic slave trade, the Wilmot Proviso, the formation of the Republican Party, and John Brown's abortive raid on the federal arsenal at Harpers Ferry. "Are we blind," he asked, "that this retrospect shall teach us no lesson?" As one New Orleans paper, critical of the South's grievance narrative, put it: secessionists "look back on the closed issues of the past . . . They seem to see but one continued series of assaults and weak defenses; one perpetual chain of concessions to be followed by those still more vital to the rights of the States, and these united in one bill of complaint are presented to the people, as an irresistible argument to stir them up to immediate and concerted resistance."[20]

Like all collective memories, the secessionist account of recent American political history was highly selective. It made no mention of the Kansas-Nebraska Act or the Buchanan administration's efforts to make Kansas a slave state against the will of the territory's free-soil majority. However, in the hands of determined politicians, the narrative proved to be a highly effective mobilizing tool, especially when linked (as it was frequently) to visceral racial fears that were themselves grounded in remembrances of past events.[21]

The radicals' insistence that "[t]he history of the Abolition or Black Republican party of the North" was "a history of repeated injuries and usurpations" was frequently coupled with demagogic assertions that the Lincoln administration would undertake policies likely to trigger slave insurrections. Memories of the Haitian slave revolt and Nat Turner's rebellion, as well as more immediate recollections of John Brown's raid, were all invoked, separately and collectively, to sharpen the secessionist narrative. Stephen F. Hale, an Alabama secession commissioner, told Governor Beriah Magoffin of Kentucky that Lincoln's election amounted to "an open declaration of war" against the South, heralding "all the horrors of a San Domingo servile insurrection, consigning her citizens to assassinations and her wives and daughters to pollution and violation to gratify the lust of half-civilized Africans." James Holcombe, a pro-secession delegate in the Virginia convention, urged his listeners to "[l]ook at the experience of the past, and take a lesson from it. The struggle between the races in St. Domingo commenced long before the enactment of the French Assembly, decreeing liberty to the blacks . . . The tragedy at Southampton, in our own State, has been traced to the influence of agitation. The John Brown raid was its offspring."[22]

Secessionists insisted that, in view of the Republicans' demonstrably fiendish plans for the region, there could be no possibility of compromise. The facts were "well known and patent," asserted one radical newspaper, and constituted a "dark record of the past": "[T]he South has compromised until she can compromise no farther." Although the editor did not say what compromises he had in mind, it is likely that he meant the abandonment of the African slave trade, the Missouri Compromise, and key elements of the 1850 Compromise, most notably the admission of California to the Union as a free state. More surrenders like this would produce a despotic Union. "The fathers of the Republic," scoffed this Louisiana fire-eater (in yet another application of Revolutionary memory) "would have spurned such a confederation with as much loathing as they did the treason of Benedict Arnold." Although some mainstream states' rights men, Jefferson Davis among them, did appear ready in December 1860 to explore the possibility of a sectional armistice based on Senator John J. Crittenden's proposal to extend the Missouri Compromise line to the Pacific, the Republicans' refusal to treat seriously with them appeared to justify the radicals' claim that no compromise with abolitionists was possible.[23]

Northern Republicans developed their own synthetic historical narrative, which, like the secessionists' variant, was often deployed to derail compromise attempts during the winter crisis. The Republicans' antislavery account of recent political history mirrored the secessionists' pro-slavery grievance narrative in combining aspects of national and regional memory. It was socially constructed—a product of inherited knowledge, lived experience, and collective self-interest. Linear in progression and sometimes suffused with belief in an immanent God, it was anchored by patriotic memories of the Revolution but strengthened, crucially, by sectional recollections of the more recent American past. Shards of the narrative appeared in many places, including the private correspondence of individual Republicans, the rhetoric of party leaders, and commentaries in the party press.

This grand antislavery narrative possessed several nodal points. It sometimes began with the three-fifths clause of the U.S. Constitution, which inflated the political power of slaveholders. Northern Federalists and Jeffersonian Republicans in the early nineteenth century had frequently cited the "federal ratio" as the reason for what they saw as their second-class status—an inferiority evidenced by the almost uninterrupted procession of Southern slaveholding presidents, all Virginians, elected between 1788 and 1820. But it derived compelling force from the assertion that an ambitious coterie of large slaveholding planters, the so-called Slave Power, had been conspiring for decades to destroy the best government on earth for its own devilish purposes.

Republicans proffered a series of allegedly interconnected political events between 1832 and 1861 as concrete and incontestable proof to support this conspiracy theory. The resulting narrative ran as follows. During the nullification crisis, South Carolinians, acting on the treasonous interposition doctrine of the planter-ideologue John C. Calhoun, had attempted to break up the Union before being thwarted temporarily by the decisive response of President Andrew Jackson. In the 1840s, Southern slaveholders led by the Virginian John Tyler and Tennessean James K. Polk had renewed the offensive by striving to expand slavery into the Far West, first by annexing Texas and then engineering a war of aggression against Mexico. When the people of the free states opposed these brazen attempts to obtain fresh land for slavery, Southerners had threatened to destroy the Union, forcing patriotic Northerners to compromise their principles by agreeing to passage of the sordid Fugitive Slave Act. This concession to the Slave Power in 1850 had merely exacerbated the South's lust for wealth and power. In 1854 its votaries (including complicit Northern dupes like the Democrat Stephen A. Douglas) ripped up the venerable Missouri Compromise and replaced it with the hated Kansas-Nebraska Act. This statute had been denounced effectively as "part and parcel of an atrocious plot" to extend slavery at the expense of freedom and prompted formation of the Republican Party as a vehicle to defend American liberty and Northern rights. Subsequent efforts by the pro-Southern administrations of Franklin Pierce and James Buchanan to spread slavery into Kansas proved the validity of the Slave Power thesis. So did calls for the reopening of the international slave trade and attempts by Southern filibusters to spread slavery beyond the boundaries of the United States. Now, at this critical moment in U.S. history, when the party of the free North had finally wrested political control of the country from the hands of the tyrannical plantocrats, Southerners were again threatening to secede in order to induce Northern acquiescence in the most craven compromise yet.[24]

As much as some felt attachment to an unbreakable Union, it was the plausibility of this Northern grievance narrative that impelled the majority of Republicans to resist calls for a bilateral settlement of the slavery question during the secession crisis—the kind of compromise that might just have given Jefferson Davis and other mainstream states' rights men reason for thought. The narrative functioned chiefly to convince most Republican leaders and activists that further compromise with slavery was positively dangerous. Compromise would demoralize the party (Republicans took it for granted that their party was integral to the future well-being of the nation) and embolden proven traitors to promote further aggressions against freedom.

Crittenden's compromise plan was the chief casualty of the Republicans' grievance narrative. Recent memories of pro-slavery expansion in the 1840s and 1850s played a critical role in determining Republican responses to the plan's most controversial provision: that slavery should be protected below an extended Missouri Compromise line in future as well as in existing territory owned by the United States. Most Republicans, at every level of the party, looked back at Southern attempts to extend the reach of slavery into the Far West, the Caribbean, and Central America and interpreted them as hard evidence of the Slave Power's expansionist designs. Francis P. Blair was a predictably vigorous opponent of Crittenden's controversial proposal. The South, insisted the Jacksonian veteran, was now seeking "conquest & extended slave empire." Whereas its politicians had nullified the Missouri Compromise in 1854 in order to spread slavery into Kansas, they now wanted to revive it to achieve the same goal on a larger scale. It was, he urged, time to stop Southerners' "game of open & shut, with these compromises." Many Republican editors made the same point to a wider audience. "Every man is acquainted with the history of the Missouri Compromise," contended an Indiana editor. "That was declared unconstitutional by the Democratic Party, and it repealed it [by passing the Kansas-Nebraska Act] . . . Shall we make another sacrifice of freedom, by another compromise, to be broken at the will of the South? The history of the Missouri Compromise teaches every intelligent man that compromise is useless."[25]

Although Lincoln and Seward, the two key Republican players during the secession crisis, were not averse to any compromise, they shared their co-partisans' predominant conviction that the Crittenden Plan meant abject surrender to the Slave Power. Seward voted against it in the Senate Committee of Thirteen, one of two congressional committees created to devise a workable solution to the secession crisis. Lincoln told Pennsylvania congressman James T. Hale that if Republicans acquiesced to slavery extension Southerners would "repeat the experiment upon us *ad libitum*. A year will not pass, till we shall have to take Cuba as a condition upon which they will stay in the Union."[26]

Stephen Douglas, the leading Northern Democrat, did support the Crittenden Plan. However, he and his allies were powerless to secure its passage without support from Republicans and Southern Democrats on the Committee of Thirteen and the House Committee of Thirty-three. The Douglasites' actions during the winter of 1860–61 were influenced by their own grievance narrative, which represented in many respects a combination of the Republican and secessionist variations. Their willingness to support compromise on Southern terms was a function of their longstanding conviction that the Republicans were John Brown supporters, crypto-abolitionists whose monomania for inferior blacks and refusal to obey the Constitution were partly responsible for the mess in which the country now found itself. As one Douglas editor in Chicago put it, "Our fathers were not Abolitionists. Our fathers executed the fugitive slave law in good faith. Our fathers neither disturbed nor sought to disturb others in the enjoyment of their rights under the law." Ultimately, however, while this historically informed view of the Republicans conditioned their attitude to compromise, it did not determine how the Douglas men responded to Southern efforts to break up the Union.[27]

The group's short-term memory of Southern betrayal in the spring and early summer of 1860 proved a determining factor in the decision of many Northern Democrats to back President Lincoln's call for troops after the attack on Fort Sumter. Douglas himself despised most of his Republican opponents and was convinced that the antislavery party's leaders "desire war & Disunion under pretext of saving the Union." His ally, the wealthy New York businessman Samuel Barlow, shared this belief, as did Barlow's influential friends, lobbyist Sam Ward and a talented *New York Times* journalist named William Henry Hurlbert. After the war, Hurlbert penned what purported to be an authentic diary of the secession crisis, the "Diary of a Public Man," in which he sought to demonstrate that war had never been inevitable in 1860–61 and implied that hardline Republicans had reinforced Sumter for partisan rather than patriotic reasons. This construction of a historical memory of the secession crisis pregnant with "what ifs" represented a conscious attempt to rebut the dogmatic postwar claims of Republican writers like Horace Greeley and Henry Wilson that Southern plantocrats were to blame for the Civil War. It drew heavily on what Hurlbert knew of the efforts of Douglas Democrats, border-state Unionists, and Secretary of State Seward to prevent a military clash between the sections. Crucially, however, most Douglasites, Hurlbert included, had set aside their reservations about cooperating with antislavery Republicans when war finally came in April 1861.[28]

One of the main reasons they did so was bitterness at Southern opposition to Douglas before and during the 1860 presidential contest. One Northern Democrat campaign pamphlet alleged that slave-state radicals like William Lowndes Yancey and Henry A. Wise had plotted to split the Democratic Party and then use the election of a Republican as an excuse to destroy the Union. "Clansmen of the

Constitution," it trumpeted, "be firm, vigilant, and united in action, that you may scatter its enemies, and preserve it inviolate from the ruthless assaults of northern fanatics as well as southern disunionists." Shortly before the November poll, the editor of the *Peoria Daily Democratic Union* inveighed against the South's manifest ingratitude toward Douglas, a national man who had always defended that region's rights under the Constitution. He denounced Southern Democrats' divisive cry for a territorial slave code as having been "conceived in sin and brought forth in iniquity." Douglas and his followers, he added, "have for years and years fought the battles of the South against the constantly increasing hordes of abolitionists." But, warned the editor, "[i]f, at a time when we still have the power to serve them and to save them, they shall consent to be led astray by designing and unprincipled aspirants to the Presidency . . . so be it!" American patriots would "frown upon the wickedness, and mock to scorn the folly, of any scheme having for its aim a dissolution of this glorious and truly God-like Union." While political self-interest and a genuine horror of civil war induced most Douglas Democrats to support compromise efforts in late 1860 and early 1861, their aversion to those Southern ultras who had shattered the Democracy as a national force and ruined their champion's presidential bid rendered them determined opponents of secession. Two days after the surrender of Sumter, the *Boston Herald* explained that Southerners had "required that Northern Democratic leaders should be sacrificed to make way for Jefferson Davis or some such man, which could not be done; hence they now find themselves without friends in the free States . . . The people of New England fought for and established American liberty, and they will defend it to the last."[29]

Emotive grievance narratives, rooted in sectionalized memories of recent American history, hampered efforts during the winter of 1860–61 to find a legislative solution to the secession crisis. But as Hurlbert's "Diary of a Public Man" clearly revealed, they did not stymie completely the efforts of Seward and Southern Unionists to stave off conflict. In the final analysis it was Abraham Lincoln's decision to reinforce the federal garrison at Fort Sumter that put paid

Abraham Lincoln and the Decision for War

Soon after he arrived in Washington, President Lincoln had been persuaded by his Machiavellian secretary of state that purposeful conciliatory efforts might keep Virginia and other Upper South states in the Union and possibly prevent the outbreak of civil war. One biographer describes him as "a willing pupil under Seward's tutelage." It is certainly true that Lincoln offered Southerners a number of olive branches during March 1861. In his inaugural he not only made his mnemonic appeal to their "better angels" but also pledged to maintain only property still in the possession of the federal government (rather than retake U.S. property that was already in Confederate hands), expressed his support for a national constitutional convention, and backed a constitutional amendment that would guarantee the security of slavery in states where it currently existed. Over the next four weeks he may have acted to quash a coercion bill drafted by Republicans in the House of Representatives and offered to withdraw Major Robert Anderson's garrison from Fort Sumter if the Virginia secession convention agreed to disperse permanently.[30]

Unsurprisingly perhaps, Seward chose to regard the president's apparent conversion to his peaceable reconstruction strategy as reason to disseminate the view that Sumter would be given up. By the second week of March, newspapers were spreading the word. The result was a storm of protest from angry Republicans who began to fear that their election victory was about to be snatched away from them. The storm soon gave way to despondency. "Every thing tends, as I have foreseen to a break-up of the Union," moaned Senator Charles Sumner of Massachusetts at the end of the month. "Things were never worse than now. But S[eward]. is infatuated." Some Democrats, by contrast, were cheered by their opponents' apparent demoralization. One Cincinnati correspondent of Tennessee Unionist Andrew Johnson reported that local Republicans were "getting pretty sore of Abe, Seward, and even [antislavery radical Salmon P.] Chase." Some people, he said, were referring to the party as having been "Tylerized," a loaded term that conjured recollections of ex-president John Tyler's attempts to break down the old Whig Party in the early 1840s.[31]

What disillusioned Republicans and bullish Democrats did not realize was that Lincoln had not turned over policy making to Seward. Although willing to explore conciliation, the new president was personally reluctant to give up any more federal forts to the Confederates. In late March he made the crucial decision—ultimately it was his alone to make—to resupply Sumter and reinforce (as well as reprovision) more defensible Fort Pickens on the Gulf coast. He chose this course of action for many reasons: time was running out, he was devoted to the Union, he feared the country's descent into South American chaos, and he knew the ridicule that would be heaped on the United States by haughty Europeans. He was aware, too, of the damage that Anderson's withdrawal would do to his administration and his party. ("Give up Sumpter, Sir," one irate New York Republican told him, "& you are as dead politically as John Brown is physically . . . Either act, immediately & decisiv[e]ly or resign & go home.") Yet it is not stretching the historical record too far to suggest that his own memories of the past also played an important role in this decision.[32]

Abraham Lincoln was a keen student of American history and politics. A former Whig, his "beau ideal of a statesman" was the Kentuckian Henry Clay, who masterminded three Union-saving compromises between 1820 and 1850. Tellingly, however, it was Clay's Unionism and not his arbitration skills that attracted Lincoln during the early weeks of the secession crisis. At home in Springfield after the election, he was apparently given to quoting from the no-nonsense speech that Clay delivered in 1850 in response to reports of secession maneuvers in South Carolina: If "the standard should be raised of open resistance to the union, and constitution and the laws, what is to be done? There can be but one possible answer: the power, the authority and dignity of the government ought to be maintained, and resistance put down at every hazard . . . the moment a daring hand is raised to resist, by force, the execution of the laws, the duty of enforcing them arises, and if the conflict which may ensue should lead to civil war, the resisting party, having begun it, will be responsible for all the consequences." When Lincoln began work on his inaugural address, Clay's speech was one of a handful of documents he requested from the private library of his law partner, William H. Herndon. The metal of Clay's speech suffused portions of the inaugural, not least his statement that "In *your* hands, my dissatisfied fellow countrymen, and not in *mine*, is the momentous issue of civil war." Given Lincoln's well-known admiration for the great Whig leader, it seems likely that his understanding of Clay's uncompromising position on secession bore heavily on his decision-making over Fort Sumter.[33]

Several of the president's acquaintances and correspondents in March 1861 drew on historical memories to advance their case for holding on to Fort Sumter. On reading reports that the administration was preparing to abandon the garrison, an outraged Francis P. Blair hurried to the White House for an interview—an action that was encouraged by a number of equally incensed Republican senators. Lincoln received him kindly, but the former Jacksonian was in no mood to hear any of the president's jokes. He told Lincoln bluntly that the surrender of the fort would be "virtually a surrender of the Union unless under irresistible force." The president, he later informed his son Montgomery, should draft a proclamation similar to that issued by Andrew Jackson in defiance of South Carolina's nullification declaration in December 1832. This edict would make clear the administration's readiness "to afford supplies & succor to the Fort" and to maintain other federal military property in the South. Added the old man, "I think there never was an occasion when an eloquent appeal by the President to the people like that of Genl Jackson in the crisis of 1832, could be of more use."[34]

A letter from James L. Hill, an Illinois Republican, on March 14 echoed Blair's attempts to harness the nullification crisis to present-day objectives. Local Republicans, Hill told Lincoln, had heard "with pain and regret" that he was considering "lowring our Glorious old Flag" in Charleston harbor. "Do you know that Genl Washington or Jackson never said 'I cant' . . . By the Eternal Fort Sumter shall be reinforced and that glorious old Flag sustained and my word for it 110,000 good and true men with Jim Hill amongst them will at once respond to the call." The following day Montgomery Blair based his lone counsel for reinforcing Sumter on the memory of Jackson's decisive response to nullification.[35]

It is likely that these ardent appeals to the president's understanding of the nullification crisis struck a chord. Lincoln was a young country storeowner in New Salem, Illinois, when South Carolina first tested the patience of the federal government. We have no record of what he thought then of the way Jackson dealt with the nullifiers. Most likely, though he was never a supporter of the proslavery general, he applauded the executive's strong nationalist response, as did many of Jackson's Whig opponents including Daniel Webster. What we do know for certain is that by late 1860 Lincoln was telling his new secretary, John G. Nicolay, that "[t]he right of a state to secede is not an open or debatable question" because it had been settled by Jackson in the 1830s. "It is the duty of the President," he said, "to execute the laws and maintain the existing Government." Little wonder that William Herndon hailed the president-elect as "Jackson redivivus" and assured the Massachusetts abolitionist Wendell Phillips that his celebrated associate would "make a grave yard of the South, if rebellion or treason lifts its head," or that Illinois's Republican governor Richard Yates confidently predicted that Lincoln would respond like Jackson if he were tested. Lincoln's conviction that the Tennessean's stern reaction to nullification must determine federal policy in the present led him to seek out a copy of Jackson's 1832 proclamation as an aid to drafting his inaugural. Although he did not mention Jackson by name on his presidential progress to Washington in February, his several hints that it might be necessary to use force against the secessionists had the authentic ring of Old Hickory about them.[36]

When the Blairs and other Republicans urged Lincoln to act like Andrew Jackson during the Sumter crisis they were clearly preaching to the converted. But the president was under intense pressure at this time to withdraw the garrison, and he came close at one point to signing an order drafted by General Winfield Scott to accomplish that end. It seems entirely likely that at this critical juncture, Lincoln's strong memory of how his hero Henry Clay and the antinullifier Andrew Jackson had responded to secession assisted his decision, implemented after a critical cabinet meeting on March 29, to sanction a relief expedition commanded by Gustavus V. Fox. Of course what Lincoln intimated in his inaugural speech was true. The "momentous decision" for war lay with Jefferson Davis's government in Montgomery. But as president of the United States it was in his power to force the Confederates' hand. And in the end his own reading of the American past and of his duty to the republic at this crossroads in its history occasioned him to do precisely that.

Memory alone cannot explain the coming of the American Civil War. Like all great conflicts this one had multiple causes. Scholars, however, have underestimated the significance of memory as a tool of political mobilization during the secession crisis. Power-seeking, ideologically driven politicians interpreted both the War of Independence and the more recent thirty years war over slavery as members of competing sections. They developed historically informed grievance narratives in order to marshal popular support for their respective positions. These narratives were constructed wittingly. They were designed to filter out inconvenient facts, rendering their polarizing accounts of American history highly selective as well as politically persuasive. The two main components of Republican memory exercised a dual influence on the Northern party's responses to secession. While the Republicans' Slave Power narrative made them hostile to the kind of comprehensive sectional compromise advocated by conservatives on both sides of the Mason-Dixon line, the sentimental creation myths of the Revolution impelled most of them to reject the idea of allowing the cotton states to depart in peace and instead to endorse a policy of coercing self-proclaimed Confederates back into the Union. Secessionists, by contrast, used their own pro-slavery grievance narrative to sever the affective ties of Union and then, for the most part, astutely positioned their would-be nation as the legitimate heir of the founders' republic. The socially constructed memories of powerful individuals played a particularly significant role during the secession winter. Abraham Lincoln's personal reading and experience of the American past induced him to equate secession with treason and to regard the Union as an unbreakable whole. If this meant civil war, he was—certainly by the first week of April 1861—fully prepared to leave the outcome to the judgment of Mars.

ROBERT J. COOK

Conclusion
❧
Conflicted Minds and Civil War Causation

THE ESSAYS IN THIS book demonstrate that the secession crisis of 1860–61 is best understood not as a single "irrepressible conflict" (to borrow the infamous phrase used by Senator William Seward in 1858) but rather as an outgrowth of multiple conflicts within the sections themselves and, indeed, within individual human actors on both sides of the Mason-Dixon line. The internal conflicts that led up to the secession of the cotton states were generated primarily by the existence of slavery. White Southerners who inhabited a republican polity marked by its fierce commitment to vigilance in defense of liberty were keenly aware that freedom was a precious attribute. However much political and religious leaders in the region might try to convince them that the slave South was, in the words of one Georgia Unionist, "a magnificent exemplification of the highest Christian excellence," they could never shed the suspicion that African Americans wanted to be free like themselves. This disturbing, often subterranean, awareness did much to drive the secessionists' urgent campaign for independence in late 1860. Unless Southerners awoke to the imminent danger of an antislavery Republican president, insisted fire-eaters like Robert B. Rhett and William L. Yancey, they would quickly find themselves deprived of the power to dominate the enslaved. The results would be devastating for white liberty and security. Slave insurrection, abolitionist-directed emancipation, the amalgamation of the races, black suffrage, black officeholders—all these terrors of the white mind would come to pass if the Southern states remained in the Union. Secession, insisted the fire-eaters, would put an end to night-time fears of murderous slaves and place a firewall—an international boundary no less—between the South and its dangerous Yankee enemies.[1]

The fire-eaters were well aware that Southern whites were a unified people in aspiration only. Secessionists themselves were divided over strategy—whether it made sense for states to leave the Union separately or collectively. They worried, not without justification, that a Republican administration would exploit tensions within the planter class and drive a wedge between slaveholders and non-slaveholders—with devastating consequences for the existing social and political order in the Deep South. A congressional ban on slavery expansion, for example, would fall harder on younger slaveholders than more established ones. Control of the federal patronage would enable the Lincoln administration to appoint non-slaveholders to local offices, weakening the political power of planter elites, and permit the dissemination of abolition propaganda through the federal mail. It was precisely because of these internal divisions and the concomitant anxiety—the most unsettling republican fear of all—that Southerners' power to influence their own lives was about to drain away, that cotton state secessionists sought to convince their white peers that disunion was the only practical remedy to Northern domination.

The slave South, however, was a disparate region. Here was the source of another internal conflict of enormous importance to the outcome of the secession crisis and to the course of the ensuing Civil War. A majority of whites in the Upper South were unconvinced by the case for secession. Even the planters of that subregion were torn over the wisdom of secession. Although they took a dim view of Black Republicans, Virginians like former president John Tyler and the future Confederate commander Robert E. Lee valued the Union in part because their own state had played a leading role in its foundation. By the time Lincoln was inaugurated president of the United States on March 4, 1861, only a minority of the slave states had joined the Confederacy.

This looked to be a heaven-sent chance to preserve the peace, to head off the appalling prospect of civil war between white Americans. Many Upper South leaders certainly thought so. Politicians like John J. Crittenden and even John Tyler himself played an active role in trying to forge a durable peace settlement that would bring the cotton states back to the national fold. (It is worth remembering that even after the first wave of secession in late 1860 and early 1861, some optimistic Americans supposed that Southern actions were intended to pressure Republicans into making a deal over slavery.) The problem confronting Upper South conservatives was that they simply did not have the power to act out their historical role as sectional mediators and determine the result of the secession crisis. Stiff-backed Republican leaders had no more intention of abandoning their opposition to slavery expansion than their Confederate opponents had any wish to remain in the Union (a point that Jefferson Davis was at pains to underline in his first speech as president of the Southern nation).[2]

William Seward, Lincoln's controversial choice as U.S. secretary of state, did possess influence in Washington and he did use it to try and keep the non-seceding slave states in the Union. His aim was laudable: to head off civil war. Holding Virginia and its sister states loyal to the government would, he supposed, seriously weaken the embryonic Confederacy and, in the short to medium term, promote a reconstruction of the Union. Seward, however, was unable to manufacture a consensus for peace. Whites in the Upper South were divided between ardent Unionists, secessionists, and conditional Unionists. The latter (of whom the tortured Robert E. Lee was a striking example) constituted the critical grouping. Conditional Unionists remained opposed to secession as long as they believed a sectional compromise was possible and the Republicans did not try to force misguided Confederates back into the Union. Seward did his utmost during the early months of 1861 to convince them that their hopes on both counts were not misplaced, but he did not control Northern public opinion or (though he thought otherwise for a time) the policy of the Lincoln administration.

The majority of ordinary Northerners were profoundly opposed to secession, but, as the responses of Benjamin Brown French revealed, they were often unsure over what to do about it once it was an accomplished fact. Many Douglas Democrats and most old-line Whigs who supported the short-lived Constitutional Union Party in the 1860 election favored offering significant concessions to the South in order to avert national disaster. Specifically, they broadly welcomed John J. Crittenden's plan to enable slavery to expand into the Western territories. This required the Republicans to relinquish the Chicago Platform on which Lincoln had been elected. Seward was willing to do this, but, hewing as they did to their Slave Power narrative of the recent past, the majority of his co-partisans would not go that far in order to mollify those whom they regarded as traitors to their country. Although President Lincoln proved sympathetic to Seward's goal of keeping the Upper South states in the Union, his immersion in Patriot history and his familiarity with Henry Clay and Andrew Jackson's stance on disunion rendered him disinclined to surrender the federal garrison at Fort Sumter—especially once it became clear, as it did during the course of March 1861, that a decision on whether to abandon or to resupply the garrison had to be made. While Lincoln's assent to the Sumter relief expedition at the end of the month signaled an end to Seward's peace policy, it did ensure that his own party would go into the impending conflict united. The Confederate attack on the fort and the president's subsequent call for troops, moreover, led the majority of Northern Democrats to rally round the flag—at least initially. The principal cost was the loss of four more slave states to the Confederacy. Many of the region's conditional Unionists, Lee included, were hardly ardent Confederates at this juncture in history, but they could not condone a military campaign against fellow Southerners led by an antislavery party that had failed to respect their time-honored influence in national counsels.

Secession and civil war were therefore manifestations not just of the breach between North and South but also of serious internal conflicts within both sections. Although it may seem strange to modern observers, many Americans in 1861 actually looked upon disunion and military force as solutions to these conflicts (which is one of the major reasons why the war broke out when it did). In supposing this they were not entirely mistaken. The experience of civil war consolidated support for the Union in the North and raised a steely Confederate nationalism in many parts of the South. Those collective narratives that politicians had used to sectionalize the country were carried into battle by the troops on both sides. Union and Confederate soldiers made clear their republican conviction that they were fighting to uphold the liberties won by their Patriot forebears and to thwart their opponents' wicked attempts either to destroy the best government on earth or to render them "slaves" to the rule of tyrants. And in the end, the war did solve the slavery question, providing a platform for the eventual reconciliation of the sections. But the shuddering recourse to violence also exacerbated many of the internal conflicts it was intended to eradicate: party conflict in the North, class tensions in both regions, internal debates of all kinds over the place of black people in society, and the ongoing struggle over the very meaning of American history. Like the secession crisis that preceded it, the Civil War was both a cause and a consequence of deeply conflicted minds.[3]

NOTES

Introduction

1. Benjamin Brown French, *Witness to the Young Republic: A Yankee's Journal, 1828–1870*, ed. Donald B. Cole and John J. McDonough (Hanover, N.H.: University Press of New England, 1989), 336–37, 338.
2. Ibid., 341, 351.
3. Henry B. Adams, "The Great Secession Winter," *Massachusetts Historical Society Proceedings* 43 (1909–10): 660–87.
4. William W. Freehling and Craig M. Simpson, eds., *Secession Debated: Georgia's Showdown in 1860* (New York: Oxford University Press, 1992), viii.
5. Bruce Levine, *Half Slave and Half Free: The Roots of Civil War* (New York: Hill and Wang, 1996), 46–94, catches the dynamism of the North's free-labor society, while Eric Foner's *Free Soil, Free Labor, Free Men: The Ideology of the Republican Party before the Civil War* (New York: Oxford University Press, 1970) analyzes the anti-Southern worldview of the Republican Party, the North's preeminent political vehicle in the second half of the 1850s.
6. Quoted in Charles Royster, "Fort Sumter: At Last the War," in Gabor S. Boritt, ed., *Why the Civil War Came* (New York: Oxford University Press, 1996), 204.
7. On the inevitability debate see David M. Potter, *Lincoln and His Party in the Secession Crisis* (New Haven: Yale University Press, 1942), Kenneth M. Stampp, *And the War Came: The North and the Secession Crisis, 1860–1861* (Baton Rouge: Louisiana State University Press, 1950), and the Guide to Further Reading in this volume.

Rush to Disaster

1. See William L. Barney, *The Secessionist Impulse: Alabama and Mississippi in 1860* (1974; repr., Tuscaloosa: University of Alabama Press, 2004), xv–xxvi for a discussion of recent work on secession.

2. For an exploration of these themes as the expression of the hidden side of master-slave relations, see Earl E. Thorpe, *The Old South: A Psychohistory* (Durham, N.C.: Seeman Printery, 1972) and, for a more clinically based analysis, Joel Kovel, *White Racism: A Psychohistory* (New York: Vintage Books, 1970).

3. A review of the historical literature on the extent to which slaveholders felt any guilt over slavery can be found in Gaines M. Foster, "Guilt Over Slavery: A Historiographical Analysis," *Journal of Southern History* 56 (Nov. 1990): 665–94. The evidence for moral unease over slavery is much more prevalent than open expressions of guilt, but whether slaveholders' attitudes are characterized as guilt or discomfort often amounts to a distinction without a difference. The line between the two is a blurred one. Thus, while avoiding any discussion of guilt, Patricia Roberts-Miller, in *Fanatical Schemes: Proslavery Rhetoric and the Tragedy of Consensus* (Tuscaloosa: University of Alabama Press, 2009), nonetheless makes a powerful case for understanding pro-slavery rhetoric in the context of an underlying moral ambiguity over slavery in which psychological needs to legitimate slavery led to the scapegoating of its perceived enemies and a defense of slavery that denied more than it reflected the actual behavior of slaveholders and the workings of slavery as an economic institution. In short, it was designed to alleviate collective frustrations and anxieties. Much the same can be said of the distinction between, on the one hand, a moral condemnation of slavery per se and, on the other, an indictment of the moral or un-Christian failings of individual slaveholders. Evangelical efforts to reform slavery, such as requiring the teaching of literacy or prohibiting the breakup of the families of slaves by sale, were blocked by slaveholders who argued that such measures would reform slavery out of existence by undercutting their near-absolute prerogatives in controlling and disposing of their slaves as they saw fit. It was not at all clear where to draw the line between meaningfully "reforming" slavery by correcting individual abuses and setting the institution on the road to eventual extinction. As a result, the acknowledged evils of slavery remained, and Christian reformers increasingly feared that they were failing to do God's will.

4. James C. Johnston to William S. Pettigrew, Jan. 1, 1861, Pettigrew Family Papers, Southern Historical Collection, University of North Carolina at Chapel Hill.

5. Letter of Benjamin F. Perry to the *Charleston Courier*, Aug. 13, 1860.

6. *New Orleans Bee*, Nov. 12, 15, 1860, and, for the last quote, Nov. 10, 1860.

7. Charles Edward Cauthen, *South Carolina Goes to War, 1860–1865* (Chapel Hill: University of North Carolina Press, 1950), 49–50; William W. Freehling, *The Road to Disunion*, vol. 2, *Secessionists Triumphant, 1854–1861* (New York: Oxford University Press, 2007), 404–5.

8. Quoted in Drew Gilpin Faust, *James Henry Hammond and the Old South: A Design for Mastery* (Baton Rouge: Louisiana State University Press, 1982), 262.

9. *Secret and Sacred: The Diaries of James Henry Hammond, a Southern Slaveholder*, ed. Carol Bleser (New York: Oxford University Press, 1988), 264.

10. James Henry Hammond to Marcus C. M. Hammond, Nov. 12, 1860, cited in *The Hammonds of Radcliffe*, ed. Carol Bleser (New York: Oxford University Press, 1981), 88.

11. On the divergent paths of the Upper and Lower South, see William W. Freehling, *The Road to Disunion*, vol. 1, *Secessionists at Bay, 1776–1854* (New York: Oxford University Press, 1990), 13–36.

12. Henry Clay to William Henry Russell, July 18, 1835, *The Papers of Henry Clay*, ed. James F. Hopkins et al., 10 vols. (Lexington: University Press of Kentucky, 1959–1992), 8:789.

13. Quoted in Freehling, *Secessionists at Bay*, 467.

14. David T. Bailey, *Shadow on the Church: Southwestern Evangelical Religion and the Issue of Slavery, 1783–1860* (Ithaca, N.Y.: Cornell University Press, 1985), 253–57.

15. Richard Fuller and Francis Wayland, *Domestic Slavery Considered as a Scriptural Institution* (New York: Lewis Colby, 1845), 170.

16. Quoted in David B. Chesebrough, *Clergy Dissent in the Old South, 1830–1865* (Carbondale and Edwardsville: Southern Illinois University Press, 1968), 31.

17. Quoted in Freehling, *Secessionists Triumphant*, 33.

18. See Richard H. Abbott, *The Republican Party and the South, 1855–1877* (Chapel Hill: University of North Carolina Press, 1986), 3–19, for these early organizational forays by the Republicans in the Border South.

19. Quoted in Roger W. Shugg, *Origins of Class Struggle in Louisiana: A Social History of White Farmers and Laborers during Slavery and After, 1840–1875* (Baton Rouge: Louisiana State University Press, 1968), 145–46.

20. *Morehouse (La.) Advocate*, cited in Frederick Law Olmsted, *A Journey in the Seaboard Slave States* (New York: Dix and Edwards, 1856), 589–90.

21. Caroline Pettigrew to James Louis Petigru, Dec. 2, [1856], Pettigrew Family Papers.

22. Charles L. Pettigrew to Caroline Pettigrew, Nov. 15, 1860, Pettigrew Family Papers.

23. Olmsted, *Journey in the Seaboard Slave States*, 675–76. T. Michael Parrish, *Richard Taylor: Soldier Prince of Dixie* (Chapel Hill: University of North Carolina Press, 1992), 46, notes that Olmsted protected Taylor's identity by referring to him in his account as "Mr. R."

24. For the Creole's views on slavery, see Olmsted, *Journey in the Seaboard Slave States*, 675–76, and for the exchange between Olmsted and William, 683–84.

25. See the review essay by Suzanne Lebsock, "Complicity and Contention: Women in the Plantation South," *Georgia Historical Quarterly* 74 (Spring 1990):

59–83, for a finely nuanced discussion of the conflicting attitudes of white plantation women regarding slavery.

26. *The Secret Eye: The Journal of Ella Gertrude Clanton Thomas, 1848–1889*, ed. Virginia Ingraham Burr, with an introduction by Nell Irvin Painter (Chapel Hill: University of North Carolina Press, 1990), 167–69. Thomas suspected her husband of infidelity with a slave mistress (see 128–29) and was convinced after the reading of her father's will in 1864 that he had willed as property to his heirs his own slave children (see 30, 231–32).

27. *Mary Chesnut's Civil War*, ed. C. Vann Woodward (New Haven, Conn.: Yale University Press, 1981), 29.

28. Quoted in Randy J. Sparks, *On Jordan's Stormy Banks: Evangelicalism in Mississippi, 1773–1876* (Athens: University of Georgia Press, 1994), 67.

29. Jeremiah Bell Jeter, *The Recollections of a Long Life* (Richmond, Va.: The Religious Herald Co., 1891), 67–71.

30. Quoted in Donald G. Mathews, *Religion in the Old South* (Chicago: University of Chicago Press, 1977), 182.

31. Quoted in Erskine Clarke, *Dwelling Place: A Plantation Epic* (New Haven, Conn.: Yale University Press, 2005), 90.

32. Rev. C. C. Jones to Mrs. Mary Jones, Dec. 10, 1856, *The Children of Pride: A True Story of Georgia and the Civil War*, ed. Robert Manson Myers (New Haven, Conn.: Yale University Press, 1972), 271.

33. Quoted in Clarke, *Dwelling Place*, 359.

34. Rev. C. C. Jones to Charles C. Jones, Jr., April 20, 1861, in Myers, ed., *The Children of Pride*, 666–67.

35. Robert L. Dabney to G. Woodson Payne, Jan. 20, 1840, cited in James Oscar Farmer, Jr., *The Metaphysical Confederacy: James Henley Thornwell and the Synthesis of Southern Values* (Macon, Ga.: Mercer University Press, 1986), 206–7.

36. William C. Preston to Waddy Thompson, Aug. 10, 1857, cited in Clement Eaton, *The Freedom-of-Thought Struggle in the Old South*, rev. ed. (New York: Harper Torchbooks, 1964), v.

37. Quoted in Francis R. Flournoy, *Benjamin Mosby Smith, 1811–1893* (Richmond: Richmond Press, 1947), 74.

38. On Nott's hatred of slavery, see his comments to William Howard Russell in Russell's *My Diary North and South*, ed. Fletcher Pratt (New York: Harper and Brothers, 1954), 127.

39. Quoted in William Stanton, *The Leopard's Spots: Scientific Attitudes toward Race in America, 1815–59* (Chicago: University of Chicago Press, 1960), 77.

40. For Thornwell's views, see Thornwell to John Adger, Dec. 10, 1856, cited in Farmer, ed., *The Metaphysical Confederacy*, 229–30.

41. Leonidas W. Spratt to John Perkins, *Charleston Mercury*, Feb. 13, 1861.

Spratt was protesting the prohibition of the African slave trade in the Confederate Constitution.

42. On this decline see Peter A. Coclanis, *The Shadow of a Dream: Economic Life and Death in the South Carolina Low Country, 1670–1920* (New York: Oxford University Press, 1989).

43. *Charleston Southern Standard*, June 25, 1853, quoted in Ronald T. Takaki, *A Pro-Slavery Crusade: The Agitation to Reopen the African Slave Trade* (New York: The Free Press, 1971), 4.

44. Quoted in Takaki, *A Pro-Slavery Crusade*, 95.

45. Eric L. McKitrick, ed., *Slavery Defended: The Views of the Old South* (Englewood Cliffs, N.J.: Prentice-Hall, 1963), 55.

46. Letter signed "St. Henry," *Jackson Semi-Weekly Mississippian*, Oct. 14, 1859, cited in Takaki, *A Pro-Slavery Crusade*, 84–85.

47. A summary of Yancey's youth and career as a radical can be found in William L. Barney, *The Road to Secession: A New Perspective on the Old South* (New York: Praeger Publishers, 1972), 86–89. For an excellent, recent biography, see Eric H. Walther, *William Lowndes Yancey and the Coming of the Civil War* (Chapel Hill: University of North Carolina Press, 2006).

48. *Speech of the Hon. William Lowndes Yancey, of Alabama: delivered in the National Democratic convention, Charleston, April 28th, 1860. With the protest of the Alabama delegation* (Charleston: Walker, Evans & Co., 1860), 4.

49. *Augusta Chronicle*, cited in *Charleston Mercury*, June 13, 1860.

50. *Augusta Dispatch*, cited in *Savannah Republican*, Aug. 13, 1860.

51. *Barnwell (S.C.) Sentinel*, cited in *Charleston Daily Courier*, Aug. 13, 1860.

52. *Newberry (S.C.) Rising Sun*, Nov. 7, 1860.

53. Frances Anne Kemble, *Journal of a Residence on a Georgian Plantation in 1838–1839*, ed. John A. Scott (Athens: University of Georgia Press, 1984), 342.

54. Amanda Edmonds Diary, Nov. 11, 1859, Virginia Historical Society, Richmond, quoted in Brenda E. Stevenson, *Life in Black and White: Family and Community in the Slave South* (New York: Oxford University Press, 1996), 322.

55. *A Plantation Mistress on the Eve of the Civil War: The Diary of Keziah Goodwyn Hopkins Brevard, 1860–1861*, ed. James Hammond Moore (Columbia: University of South Carolina Press, 1993), Oct. 13, 1860, 38; Jan. 8, 1861, 70; Feb. 13, 1861, 90; Jan. 8, 1861, 70; April 4, 1861, 111; April 13, 1861, 115.

56. *Charleston Mercury*, June 14, 1860.

57. Ibid.

58. For the flags and the themes they expressed, see the *Charleston Mercury* and the *Charleston Daily Courier* for November 1860.

59. Letter from "More Anon," *Charleston Mercury*, Nov. 13, 1860.

60. Rev. Benjamin Morgan Palmer, "The South: Her Peril and Her Duty," in

Southern Pamphlets on Secession, November 1860–April 1861, ed. Jon L. Wakelyn (Chapel Hill: University of North Carolina Press, 1996), 66, 67, 71, 69, 77.

61. Caroline Pettigrew to Charles L. Pettigrew, Nov. 17, 1860, Pettigrew Family Papers.

62. Charles Manigault to Louis Manigault, Jan. 19, 1861, in *Life and Labor on Argyle Island: Letters and Documents of a Savannah River Plantation, 1833–1867*, ed. James M. Clifton (Savannah, Ga.: The Beehive Press, 1978), 313.

63. *Newberry (S.C.) Rising Sun*, Jan. 23, 1861.

"Save in Defense of My Native State"

1. On Jan. 22, 1861, Lee wrote his cousin Martha Custis Williams: "If a disruption takes place, I shall go back in sorrow to my people & share the misery of my native state, & save in her defense there will be one soldier less in the world than there is now." Avery Craven, ed., *"To Markie": The Letters of Robert E. Lee to Martha Custis Williams* (Cambridge: Harvard University Press, 1933), 58–59. For Lee's April 20, 1861, letters to Scott, to his sister Anne, and to his brother Sydney—all of which feature his "save in the defense of my native state" formulation, see Robert E. Lee, Jr., ed., *Recollections and Letters* (1904; repr., New York: Barnes & Noble, 2004), 18–20.

2. Douglas Southall Freeman, *R. E. Lee: A Biography*, 4 vols. (New York: Charles Scribner's Sons, 1934–1935), 1:431, 440, 447; Alan T. Nolan, *Lee Considered: General Robert E. Lee and Civil War History* (Chapel Hill: University of North Carolina Press, 1991), 47, 49, 57; Emory M. Thomas, *Robert E. Lee: A Biography* (New York: W. W. Norton, 1995), 80, 189; Michael Fellman, *The Making of Robert E. Lee* (Baltimore: Johns Hopkins University Press, 2000), 76, 85, 89; Brian Holden Reid, *Robert E. Lee: Icon for a Nation* (London: Weidenfeld & Nicholson, 2005), 62; Elizabeth Brown Pryor, *Reading the Man: A Portrait of Robert E. Lee Through His Private Letters* (New York: Penguin, 2007), 285–87, 297.

3. On disunion accusations as a staple of anti-abolition rhetoric, see Elizabeth R. Varon, *Disunion! The Coming of the American Civil War, 1789–1859* (Chapel Hill: University of North Carolina Press, 2008), 87–124.

4. Varon, *Disunion!*, 45, 116–20; Judge [Nathaniel] Beverley Tucker, *The Partisan Leader: A Novel, and an Apocalypse of the Origin and Struggles of the Southern Confederacy*, ed. Thomas Ware (1836; repr., Richmond: West and Johnson, 1862).

5. Varon, *Disunion!*, 223–24, 237.

6. William Link, *The Roots of Secession: Slavery and Politics in Antebellum Virginia* (Chapel Hill: University of North Carolina Press, 2003), 220–23; Varon, *Disunion!*, 339–40; William W. Freehling and Craig M. Simpson, eds., *Showdown in Virginia: The 1861 Convention and the Fate of the Union* (Charlottesville: University of Virginia

Press, 2010), 34; *New York Times*, Dec. 11, 1860; John Minor Botts, *Union or Disunion. The Union Cannot and Shall Not Be Dissolved* (Lynchburg: n.p., 1860), 23.

7. Freehling and Simpson, eds., *Showdown in Virginia*, 14, 18, 20–21, 26, 28–29, 32, 41, 47, 82, 84.

8. Varon, *Disunion!*, 287–94.

9. On the allegations that Seward's speech sparked Brown's raid, see ibid., 330–33.

10. *Speech of Hon. Roger A. Pryor of Virginia, on the Principles and Policy of the Black Republican Party* (Washington, D.C.: Congressional Globe Office, 1859), 11–14.

11. William W. Freehling and Craig M. Simpson, eds., *Secession Debated: Georgia's Showdown in 1860* (New York: Oxford University Press, 1992), 10, 55–58, 68, 103, 115, 120.

12. Ibid., 72, 128–29; Wise speech, April 6, 1861, "Secession: Virginia and the Crisis of Union, 1861," University of Richmond Libraries, http://collections.richmond.edu/secession (hereafter "Virginia Secession Convention, UR").

13. *Staunton Vindicator*, March 22, 1860.

14. On the themes of secession as revolution, the perpetual union, and Northern disunionism, see Robert E. Lee to Annette Carter, Jan. 16, 1861, Robert E. Lee Papers, Special Collections, Washington and Lee University, Lexington, Virginia, and the transcript of Lee's Jan. 29, 1861, letter to Rooney, in William M. E. Rachal, ed., "'Secession Is Nothing but Revolution': A Letter of R. E. Lee to His Son 'Rooney,'" *Virginia Magazine of History and Biography* 69 (Jan. 1961): 2–6. On the theme of Providence, see Lee's Dec. 14, 1860, letter to G. W. Custis Lee, in J. W. Jones, *Life and Letters of Gen. Robert Edward Lee, Soldier and Man* (1906; repr., Harrisonburg, Va.: Sprinkle Publications, 1986), 119, and his Jan. 22, 1861, letter to his cousin Martha in Craven, ed., *"To Markie,"* 58–59.

15. For Lee's condemnation of Deep South radicalism, see his Dec. 14, 1860, letter to Custis Lee, in Jones, *Life and Letters of Gen. Robert Edward Lee*, 119.

16. Craven, ed., *"To Markie,"* 58–59; Jones, *Life and Letters of Gen. Robert Edward Lee*, 121–22; Rachal, ed., "'Secession Is Nothing but Revolution,'" 2–6.

17. On pro-slavery Unionism and the Federalist/Whig tradition, see Varon, *Disunion!* On professional soldiers' belief that they should disdain open politicking, see Thomas J. Goss, *The War within the Union High Command: Politics and Generalship during the Civil War* (Lawrence: University Press of Kansas, 2003). On Madison's theory of the affective Union, see Rogan Kersh, *Dreams of a More Perfect Union* (Ithaca, N.Y.: Cornell University Press, 2001). On secession as folly and disunion as an ordeal, see Lee to Annette Carter, Jan. 16, 1861, Lee Papers, Washington and Lee; Jones, *Life and Letters of Gen. Robert Edward Lee*, 122; and Craven, ed., *"To Markie,"* 58–59.

18. On the public nature of Lee's decision, see newspaper accounts of rumors

of his resignation, which began circulating six weeks before he made his choice known: *Richmond Dispatch*, Feb. 8, 1861; *Alexandria Gazette*, as quoted by *Richmond Daily Dispatch*, April 26, 1861; *Franklin (Pa.) Valley Spirit*, March 6, 1861; *The Liberator*, March 8, 1861; *Philadelphia Inquirer*, April 8, 1861.

19. *Lynchburg Virginian*, quoted in Henry T. Shanks, *The Secession Movement in Virginia, 1847–1861* (New York: AMS Press, 1934), 199–200; Daniel W. Crofts, *Reluctant Confederates: Upper South Unionists in the Secession Crisis* (Chapel Hill: University of North Carolina Press, 1989), 335–39.

20. Early and Wise speeches, April 17–19, 1861, Virginia Secession Convention, UR; Thomas, *Robert E. Lee*, 188–89; Link, *Roots of Secession*, 242–43.

21. Lee's April 20, 1861, letter to his sister Anne Marshall, in Lee, Jr., ed., *Recollections and Letters*, 20.

22. Mary Custis Lee to Rev. R. R. Gurley, [April] 1861, typescript in Special Collections, Alderman Library, University of Virginia; George C. Kundahl, *Alexandria Goes to War: Beyond Robert E. Lee* (Knoxville: University of Tennessee Press, 2004), 25–27; James D. McCabe, Jr., *Life and Campaigns of General Robert E. Lee* (Atlanta: National Publishing Company, 1866), 29–30.

23. Thomas, *Robert E. Lee*, 188; John S. Mosby, *Mosby's Memoirs: The Memoirs of John Singleton Mosby*. Introduction by Ben Wynne (1917; repr., New York: Barnes & Noble, 2006), 238–39; Freeman, *R. E. Lee*, 1: 436–42.

24. Lee, Jr., ed., *Recollections and Letters*, 19–20.

25. Ibid., 18–20.

26. Mary Custis Lee to Gurley, [April] 1861, UVa; "Memoir of Mrs. Harriotte Lee Taliaferro Concerning Events in Virginia, Apr. 11–21, 1861," *Virginia Magazine of History and Biography* 57 (Oct. 1949): 419.

27. On antebellum Virginians' nostalgia for the past, see Susan Dunn, *Dominion of Memories: Jefferson, Madison, and the Decline of Virginia* (New York: Basic Books, 2007), 5, 12, 14, 19, 44, 83–84, 126. For Janney quote, see *New York Times*, Nov. 6, 1862.

28. On Lee's reverence for Washington, see Richard B. McCaslin, *Lee in the Shadow of Washington* (Baton Rouge: Louisiana State University Press, 2007).

29. Freeman, *R. E. Lee*, 1:446–49.

30. Harvie speeches, April 20, 22, 1861, Virginia Secession Convention, UR.

31. Macfarland and Harvie speeches, April 22, 1861, Virginia Secession Convention, UR; Link, *Roots of Secession*, 226.

32. Macfarland speech, April 22, 1861, Virginia Secession Convention, UR.

33. Early, Critcher, Harvie, and Hall speeches, April 22, 1861, Virginia Secession Convention, UR.

34. *Richmond Daily Dispatch*, April 23, 1861; Thomas, *Robert E. Lee*, 191.

35. Macfarland and Sheffey speeches, April 22, 1861, Virginia Secession Convention, UR.

36. On Janney, see Nelson D. Lankford, *Cry Havoc! The Crooked Road to Civil War, 1861* (New York: Viking, 2007), 46, 51, 59, 103, 114, 118, 123, 240; Janney speech, April 18, 1861, Virginia Secession Convention, UR.

37. Janney and Lee speeches, April 23, 1861, Virginia Secession Convention, UR. For a press account of the convention proceedings, see, for example, *Staunton Spectator*, April 30, 1861.

38. Henry Cleveland, *Alexander H. Stephens, in Public and Private: With Letters and Speeches, before, during, and since the War* (Philadelphia: National Publishing Company, 1866), 717–29; Stephens speech, April 23, 1861, Virginia Secession Convention, UR.

39. Cleveland, *Alexander H. Stephens*, 717–29; Stephens speech, April 23, 1861, Virginia Secession Convention, UR.

40. Cleveland, *Alexander H. Stephens*, 717–29; Stephens speech, April 23, 1861, Virginia Secession Convention, UR.

41. Macfarland speech, April 23, 1861, Virginia Secession Convention, UR. On press reactions to Lee's decision, see, for example, *Richmond Dispatch*, April 23, 1861; *Lynchburg Virginian*, as quoted in *Macon Telegraph*, April 29, 1861; *New Orleans Daily True Delta*, May 5, 1861; *Dallas Weekly Herald*, June 5, 1861. For the Chesnut quotation, see Isabella D. Martin and Myrta Lockett Avary, eds., *A Diary from Dixie* (New York: D. Appleton & Co., 1905), 424.

42. On Lee's apotheosis as the symbol of Confederate nationalism, see Gary W. Gallagher, *The Confederate War* (Cambridge: Harvard University Press, 1999); *Lee and His Army in Confederate History* (Chapel Hill: University of North Carolina Press, 2001); Gallagher, ed., *Lee the Soldier* (Lincoln: University of Nebraska Press, 1996).

43. Bledsoe and Pollard, as quoted in Thomas, *Robert E. Lee*, 197, 209; *Wisconsin Daily Patriot*, July 6, 1861; *Macon Telegraph*, July 16, 1861; *Richmond Dispatch*, June 11, 1861; Reid, *Robert E. Lee*, 68–69.

44. Freeman, *R. E. Lee*, 1:447.

45. For Early's postwar account of Lee's decision, see Jubal A. Early, "The Campaigns of Gen. Robert E. Lee," in Gallagher, ed., *Lee the Soldier*, 38–39.

46. Russell F. Weigley, *A Great Civil War: A Military and Political History, 1861–1865* (Bloomington: Indiana University Press, 2000), xxvii.

47. *New York Herald* story, reprinted in *Lancaster Intelligencer*, May 3, 1865.

48. Ibid.

The Shadow of the Past

1. Steven Watts, *The Republic Reborn: War and the Making of Liberal America* (Baltimore: Johns Hopkins University Press, 1987); Drew R. McCoy, *The Last of*

the Fathers: James Madison and the Republican Legacy (Cambridge, UK: Cambridge University Press, 1989), 73–76, 140–41.

2. Peter S. Carmichael, *The Last Generation: Young Virginians in Peace, War, and Reunion* (Chapel Hill: University of North Carolina Press, 2005); McCoy, *Last of the Fathers*, 253–322.

3. Abraham Lincoln, speech of Oct. 27, 1854, in Roy P. Basler, ed., *The Collected Works of Abraham Lincoln*, 9 vols. (New Brunswick: Rutgers University Press, 1953–1955), 2: 275. The controversial Kansas-Nebraska Act opened up Western territory to slavery expansion and led directly to the formation of the Republican Party as a vehicle to protect Northern interests. William E. Gienapp, *The Origins of the Republican Party 1852–1856* (New York: Oxford University Press, 1987), 69–102 and ff.

4. Maurice Halbwachs, *On Collected Memory*, ed. Lewis A. Coser (Chicago: University of Chicago Press, 1992), 54. Bill Schwartz and Susanna Redstone, *Memory: Histories, Theories, Debates* (New York: Fordham University Press, 2010) is a useful introduction to the development and application of memory as an intellectual concept.

5. John Bodnar, *Remaking America: Public Memory, Commemoration, and Patriotism in the Twentieth Century* (Princeton: Princeton University Press, 1992) is instructive on the distinction between official and unofficial ("vernacular") memories. On counter-memory, see David W. Blight, "W. E. B. Du Bois and the Struggle for American Historical Memory," in Geneviève Fabre and Robert O'Meally, eds., *History and Memory in African-American Culture* (New York: Oxford University Press, 1994), 46. The efforts of black and white abolitionists to construct their own narrative of the Revolution are explored in Mitch Kachun, "From Forgotten Founder to Indispensable Icon: Crispus Attucks, Black Citizenship, and Collective Memory, 1770–1865," *Journal of the Early Republic* 29 (Summer 2009): 249–86, and Margot Minardi, *Making Slavery History: Abolitionism and the Politics of Memory in Massachusetts* (New York: Oxford University Press, 2010), 132–64.

6. Simon Cameron to Lincoln, March 16, 1861; Edward Bates to Lincoln, March 15, 1861; Montgomery Blair to Lincoln, March 15, 1861, Abraham Lincoln Papers, Library of Congress.

7. Jill Lapore, *The Whites of Their Eyes: The Tea Party's Revolution and the Battle over American History* (Princeton: Princeton University Press, 2010).

8. *Charleston Mercury*, July 25, 1860, in Dwight L. Dumond, ed., *Southern Editorials on Secession* (New York: The Century Co., 1931), 153.

9. Thomas R. R. Cobb, speech of Nov. 12, 1860, in William W. Freehling and Craig M. Simpson, eds., *Secession Debated: Georgia's Showdown in 1860* (New York: Oxford University Press, 1992), 14.

10. Benjamin H. Hill, speech of Nov. 15, 1860, in Freehling and Simpson, eds.,

Secession Debated, 88, 90; Alexander H. Stephens to J. Henly Smith, Sept. 16, 1860, in Ulrich Bonnell Phillips, ed., *The Correspondence of Robert Toombs, Alexander H. Stephens, and Howell Cobb* (1911; repr., New York: Da Capo Press, 1970), 499; Alexander H. Stephens, speech of Nov. 14, in Freehling and Simpson, eds., *Secession Debated*, 57.

11. Andrew Johnson, speech on secession, Dec. 18–19, 1860, in LeRoy P. Graf and Ralph W. Haskins, eds., *The Papers of Andrew Johnson*, 17 vols., 1860–1861 (Knoxville: University of Tennessee Press, 1976), 4:5, 35; William W. Freehling and Craig M. Simpson, eds., *Showdown in Virginia: The 1861 Convention and the Fate of the Union* (Charlottesville: University of Virginia Press, 2010), 184.

12. Cobb, speech of Nov. 12, 1860, in Freehling and Simpson, eds., *Secession Debated*, 9; Harris quoted in Charles B. Dew, *Apostles of Disunion: Southern Secession Commissioners and the Causes of the Civil War* (Charlottesville: University of Virginia Press, 2001), 29. On the *Dred Scott* case see David M. Potter, *The Impending Crisis, 1848–1861* (New York: Harper Torchbooks, 1976), 267–96.

13. David Armitage, "Secession and Civil War," in Don H. Doyle, ed., *Secession as an International Phenomenon: From America's Civil War to Contemporary Secessionist Movements* (Athens: University of Georgia Press, 2010), 48; Davis, "Farewell Address," Jan. 21, 1861, in Lynda Lasswell Crist, ed., *The Papers of Jefferson Davis*, 13 vols. to date (Baton Rouge: Louisiana State University Press, 1971–2012), 7:22; Davis, "Inaugural Address," Feb. 18, 1861, ibid., 46; William C. Davis, *Jefferson Davis: The Man and His Hour* (New York: Harper Collins, 1991), 313. On the derivative nature of the Confederate Constitution and early national symbols, see Emory M. Thomas, *The Confederate Nation, 1861–1865* (New York: Harper and Row, 1979), 57–58, 63; Drew Gilpin Faust, *The Creation of Confederate Nationalism: Ideology and Identity in the Civil War South* (Baton Rouge: Louisiana State University Press, 1989), 14; George C. Rable, *The Confederate Republic: A Revolution against Politics* (Chapel Hill: University of North Carolina Press, 1994), 46–49; Anne Sarah Rubin, *A Shattered Nation: The Rise and Fall of the Confederacy, 1861–1868* (Chapel Hill: University of North Carolina Press, 2005), 14–25.

14. Harold Holzer, *Lincoln at Cooper Union: The Speech That Made Abraham Lincoln President* (New York: Simon & Schuster, 2004); Lincoln, remarks to New Jersey senate, in Basler, ed., *Collected Works*, 4:235–36.

15. *Morning Courier and New-York Enquirer*, Jan. 8, 1861, in Howard Cecil Perkins, ed., *Northern Editorials on Secession*, 2 vols. (1942; repr., Gloucester, Mass.: Peter Smith, 1964), 2:931, 932, 933–34, 935, 937.

16. "A Citizen of New York City" to Johnson, Dec. 19, 1860, in Graf and Haskins, eds., *Papers of Andrew Johnson*, 4:53; Mary Hancock Colyer to Lincoln, March 22, 1861, Lincoln Papers.

17. *Troy Daily Whig*, April 4, 1861, in Perkins ed., *Northern Editorials*, 2:670, 671.

18. Francis P. Blair, Sr., to Lincoln, Jan. 14, 1861, Lincoln Papers; William H. Seward to Lincoln, March 15, 1861, ibid.

19. Lincoln, first inaugural address, in Basler, ed., *Collected Works*, 4:271.

20. Cobb, speech of Nov. 12, 1860, in Freehling and Simpson, eds., *Secession Debated*, 16, 19; *New Orleans Daily Picayune*, Nov. 4, 1860, in Dumond, ed., *Southern Editorials*, 215.

21. The attempts of successive Democratic administrations to side with pro-slavery forces in the Kansas Territory are surveyed in Potter, *Impending Crisis*, 199–224, 297–327.

22. *New Orleans Daily Crescent*, Nov. 13, 1860, in Dumond, ed., *Southern Editorials*, 236; Stephen F. Hale to Beriah Magoffin, Dec. 27, 1860, in Dew, *Apostles of Disunion*, 98; Freehling and Simpson, eds., *Showdown in Virginia*, 66.

23. For a concise account of the 1850 Compromise see Potter, *Impending Crisis*, 90–120; *New Orleans Daily Crescent*, Nov. 13, 1860, in Dumond, ed., *Southern Editorials*, 236, 237.

24. "Appeal of the Independent Democrats," quoted in Robert Cook, *Civil War America: Making a Nation, 1848–1877* (Harlow, UK: Pearson Education, 2003), 76.

25. Blair to Lincoln, Jan. 14, 1861, Lincoln Papers. Crittenden's compromise measures are detailed in Kenneth M. Stampp, *And the War Came: The North and the Secession Crisis, 1860–1861* (Baton Rouge: Louisiana State University Press, 1950), 129–30; *Muncie Eastern Indiana Courant*, Jan. 3, 1861, in Perkins, ed., *Northern Editorials*, 1:290.

26. Lincoln quoted in Michael Burlingame, *Abraham Lincoln: A Life*, 2 vols. (Baltimore: Johns Hopkins University Press, 2008), 1:714.

27. *Chicago Daily Times and Herald*, Nov. 21, 1860, in Perkins, ed., *Northern Editorials*, 1:95.

28. Stephen A. Douglas to Charles H. Lanphier, Dec. 25 1860, in Robert V. Johannsen, ed., *The Letters of Stephen A. Douglas* (Urbana: University of Illinois Press, 1961), 504; Daniel W. Crofts, *A Secession Crisis Enigma: William Henry Hurlbert and "The Diary of a Public Man"* (Baton Rouge: Louisiana State University Press, 2010).

29. "The Conspiracy to Break Up the Union," in Joel H. Silbey, ed., *The American Party Battle: Election Campaign Pamphlets 1828–1876*, 2 vols. (Cambridge: Harvard University Press, 1999), 2:113; *Peoria Daily Democratic Union*, Oct. 5, 1860, in Perkins, ed., *Northern Editorials*, 1: 49–50; *Boston Herald*, April 15, 1861, in ibid., 2:731.

30. Burlingame, *Abraham Lincoln*, 2:45.

31. Charles Sumner to John Jay, March 27, 1861, in Beverly Wilson Palmer, ed., *The Selected Letters of Charles Sumner*, 2 vols. (Boston: Northeastern University

Press, 1990), 2:62; James R. Hood to Johnson, March 17, 1861, in Graf and Haskins, eds., *Papers of Andrew Johnson*, 4:402.

32. "A Republican" to Lincoln, April 3, 1861, Lincoln Papers.

33. Quoted in Burlingame, *Abraham Lincoln*, 1:757; Lincoln, first inaugural address, in Basler, ed., *Collected Works*, 4:261.

34. Burlingame, *Abraham Lincoln*, 2:101; Blair to Montgomery Blair, March 12, 1861, Lincoln Papers.

35. James L. Hill to Lincoln, March 14, 1861, Lincoln Papers.

36. Quoted in David Donald, *Lincoln* (1995; repr., London: Pimlico, 1996), 269; quoted in Burlingame, *Abraham Lincoln*, 1: 685; Russell McClintock, *Lincoln and the Decision for War: The Northern Response to Secession* (Chapel Hill: University of North Carolina Press, 2008), 54.

Conclusion

1. Benjamin H. Hill, speech of Nov. 15, 1860, quoted in William W. Freehling and Craig M. Simpson, eds., *Secession Debated: Georgia's Showdown in 1860* (New York: Oxford University Press, 1992), 93.

2. Reconstruction of the Union, Jefferson Davis pronounced in his inaugural address in Montgomery, was "neither practicable nor desirable." Davis, inaugural address, Feb. 18, 1861, in Lynda Lasswell Crist, ed., *The Papers of Jefferson Davis*, 13 vols. to date (Baton Rouge: Louisiana State University Press, 1971–2012), 7:49.

3. David W. Blight, *Race and Reunion: The Civil War in American Memory* (Cambridge: Belknap Press of Harvard University Press, 2001) is the best modern introduction to the war's impact on historical memory in the late nineteenth and early twentieth centuries.

GUIDE TO
FURTHER READING

❦

The central role played by the secession crisis in the coming of the Civil War has rendered it the focus of many rewarding works of historical scholarship. Useful narratives of the crisis written for a popular market—books such as Bruce Catton's characteristically evocative *The Coming Fury* (1961), Maury Klein's *Days of Defiance: Sumter, Secession, and the Coming of the Civil War* (1997), and Nelson D. Lankford's *Cry Havoc! The Crooked Road to Civil War, 1861* (2007)—should be read in conjunction with other texts in order to contextualize secession and its aftermath. Leonard L. Richards's *The Slave Power: The Free North and Southern Domination, 1780–1860* (2000), Matthew Mason's *Slavery and Politics in the Early Republic* (2006), and Elizabeth R. Varon's *Disunion! The Coming of the American Civil War* (2008) demonstrate in different ways that the South's peculiar institution was a divisive factor in American politics long before the guns opened up on Fort Sumter, while Michael F. Holt's influential *The Political Crisis of the 1850s* (1978) shows how the development of a national party system functioned to contain the political damage caused by debates over slavery in the antebellum period. The divisive issue of whether slavery should be allowed to expand into the territories is covered insightfully by Michael A. Morrison in his *Slavery and the American West: The Eclipse of Manifest Destiny and the Coming of the Civil War* (1997).

Michael Holt and William E. Gienapp are the two leading authorities on the collapse of the second-party system, an understanding of which is essential for anyone trying to come to terms with the demise of consensus in the United States. Holt's *The Rise and Fall of the American Whig Party* (1999) is an epic work of scholarship that charts in impressive detail the destruction of one of the main bulwarks of the antebellum republic. His *The Fate of Their Country: Politicians, Slavery Extension, and the Coming of the Civil War* (2004) is more accessible although coverage of the second half of the 1850s is thin. Gienapp's *The Origins of the Republican Party, 1852–1856* (1987) is a detailed analysis of the emergence of a Northern sectional party in the mid-1850s which is backed up by an impressive amount of quantitative date. Eric Foner's timeless classic, *Free Soil, Free Labor, Free Men: The Ideology of the Republican Party before the Civil War* (1970), makes a strong case for viewing moral opposition to slavery as an important component of Republicanism and ably pinpoints the threat that the new party posed to slaveholding Southerners during this critical decade. David M. Potter's *The Impending Crisis, 1848–1861* (1976), Bruce Collins's *The Origins of America's Civil War* (1981), and Bruce Levine's *Half Slave and Half Free: The Roots of Civil War* (1992) rank as the most stimulating, single-volume overviews of a turbulent decade that nearly culminated in the destruction of the United States.

The cotton South's response to the rise of the Republican Party receives rewarding treatment in a number of texts, most of which stress the determination of the region's politicians to defend their slave-based society against perceived aggression by the North. These include Steven A. Channing's *Crisis of Fear: Secession in South Carolina* (1970), Manisha Sinha's *The Counterrevolution of Slavery: Politics and Ideology in Antebellum South Carolina* (2000), and William W. Freehling's *The Road to Disunion*, vol. 2, *Secessionists Triumphant, 1854–1861* (2007). Freehling's sparkling text is the fullest and sharpest account to date of how radical secessionists, a relatively marginal grouping in the early 1850s, managed to achieve their revolutionary aims in the wake of Lincoln's election victory. He is particularly adept at demonstrating the significance of contingent events in this process, a factor that is also highlighted in Eric H. Walther's *William Lowndes Yancey and the Coming of the Civil War* (2006), the most illuminating modern biography of a Southern fire-eater. While Charles B. Dew's concise *Apostles of Disunion: Southern Secession Commissioners and the Causes of the Civil War* (2001) confirms that fear of blacks was a powerful mobilizing force in Southern secession, Michael P. Johnson's *Toward a Patriarchal Republic: The Secession of Georgia* (1977) reminds us that class divisions between slaveholders and non-slaveholders exercised a crucial role in the thinking of secessionist politicians. Evidence that white Southerners' attachment to a patriarchal honor code also influenced political behavior can be found in Christopher J. Olsen's *Political Culture and Secession in Mississippi: Masculinity, Honor, and the Antiparty Tradition, 1830–1860* (2000) and Shearer Davis Bowman's *At the Precipice: Americans North and South during the Secession Crisis* (2010). William L. Barney's *The Secessionist Impulse: Alabama and Mississippi in 1860* (1974; reprint 2004) and J. Mills Thornton, III's *Power and Politics in a Slave Society: Alabama 1800–1860* (1978) are two particularly important state studies of secession. Whereas Barney sees friction between older, established planters and young, ambitious slaveholders as a key factor in secession, Thornton focuses attention on ordinary Southern whites' commitment to personal independence and their long-standing suspicion of external power sources.

Ralph A. Wooster's *The Secession Conventions of the South* (1962) is dated but it remains the best state-by-state treatment of the political process by which the Deep South abandoned the Union—a fact that highlights the urgent need for a comprehensive modern history of the secession movement. One of the most incisive and persuasive assessments can be found in Stephanie McCurry's *Confederate Reckoning: Power and Politics in the Civil War South* (2010), which follows Freehling in stressing the contingent nature of the disunion process in the Deep South as well as the radicals' frequent recourse to intimidation. Readers wishing to embark on their own synthesis will find an abundance of printed primary materials available, notably: Dwight Lowell Dumond, ed., *Southern Editorials on Secession* (1931); Jon L. Wakelyn, ed., *Southern Pamphlets on Secession, November 1860–April 1861* (1996); and William W. Freehling and Craig M. Simpson, eds., *Secession Debated: Georgia's Showdown in 1860* (1992) and *Showdown in Virginia: The 1861 Convention and the Fate of the Union* (2010).

It is important to remember that Southern whites were far from united in their response to Lincoln's election, a point that is driven home in William Freehling's myth-busting *The South vs. the South: How Anti-Confederate Southerners Shaped the Course of the Civil War* (2001). The literature on Southern states' rights moderates and Unionists of all stripes is disappointingly thin, but Thomas E. Schott's *Alexander H. Stephens of Georgia: A Biography* (1987) and Elizabeth Brown Pryor's *Reading the Man: A Portrait of Robert E. Lee Through His Private Letters* (2007) can be mined for relevant insights. By far the most valuable book on this subject, however, is Daniel W. Crofts's *Reluctant Confederates: Upper South Unionists in the Secession Crisis* (1989), an outstanding contribution to the literature on the secession crisis. Charting the efforts of conservatives in Virginia and other non-seceding states to broker a peaceful solution to the sectional imbroglio, Crofts suggests that different actions might have prevented civil war.

Much scholarly debate over the secession crisis in fact has been concerned with the question of whether conflict between North and South was inevitable in 1861. The best place to start here is David M. Potter's *Lincoln and His Party in the Secession Crisis* (1942; reprint 1962, 1995), a major influence on Crofts's canonical text. Although somewhat dated and under-researched, it is the work of one of the most accomplished American historians of his or any other generation. The book exemplified the author's determination to avoid judgments based on hindsight. War might have been prevented, intimated Potter, if the Republicans had not made the mistake of dismissing secession as bluster and overestimating the strength of Southern Unionism. This thesis was rebutted in Kenneth M. Stampp's *And the War Came: The North and the Secession Crisis, 1860–1861* (1950), still the starting point for much modern work on this decisive moment in American history. On the basis of more extensive manuscript research than Potter, Stampp contended that war was virtually inevitable in view of the Republicans' determination (a determination with which Stampp broadly sympathized) to place slavery on the road to extinction. This text remained the standard account of the crisis until Russell McClintock's *Lincoln and the Decision for War: The Northern Response to Secession* was published in 2008. McClintock's well-argued and finely grained text constitutes a significant updating of Stampp's interpretation. Although the author broadly endorses

Stampp's contention (shared with Potter) that the crisis must be understood primarily in terms of high politics, he provides a much more convincing account of the relationship between Republican politicians and the Northern public. Abraham Lincoln's resolute and representative opposition to the kind of compromise that would have satisfied mainstream Southern leaders like Jefferson Davis, contends McClintock, was highly likely to trigger civil war.

The fate of the various compromise efforts are reviewed by Potter in the latter stages of his *Impending Crisis*. We lack modern biographies of some of the principal compromisers, however, not least John J. Crittenden, whose comprehensive plan of sectional adjustment not only offered the best hope for keeping the peace but also merits a book of its own. Robert Gray Gunderson's *Old Gentlemen's Convention: The Washington Peace Conference of 1861* (1961), remains the standard account of the February 1861 peace convention, an ill-fated gathering that is normally, yet perhaps unhelpfully, dismissed as irrelevant by scholars of this period. Although no comprehensive analysis of William Seward's peace policy exists, the New Yorker's increasingly desperate efforts to stave off war and keep the Upper South states in the Union can be tracked partially in Crofts's *Reluctant Confederates*. The same author's *A Secession Crisis Enigma: William Henry Hurlbert and "The Diary of a Public Man"* (2010) is an intriguing piece of historical detective work. Crofts uncovers the author of a sensational postbellum account that, partly fictionalized though it was, casts doubt on simplistic notions that war was bound to break out in 1861. Seward appears as an optimistic figure in "The Diary of a Public Man," the text of which is usefully reprinted for modern readers in Crofts's book.

Northern popular responses to the crisis have not received adequate treatment from historians. In many respects the best introduction to this topic is Howard C. Perkins's useful collection of primary materials, *Northern Editorials on Secession* (2 vols., 1942; reprint 1964). Newspaper editors were highly partisan observers of events, but the populace itself was heavily politicized in 1860-61. This was true of African Americans no less than whites, as evidenced by David W. Blight's *Frederick Douglass' Civil War: Keeping Faith in Jubilee* (1989). Notwithstanding its primary focus on the actions of political elites, Russell McClintock's *Lincoln and the Decision for War* evinces greater awareness than most studies of the symbiotic relationship that pertained between politicians and ordinary Northerners. Northern Democrats have not been well served by scholars, although Philip S. Klein's *President James Buchanan* (1962) and Robert W. Johannsen's *Stephen A. Douglas* (1973) remain useful studies. The views of influential Republican leaders (who were largely though by no means unanimously hostile to Seward's compromise efforts) can be discerned by consulting the works in the next paragraph as well as biographies of key politicians. See, for example, David Herbert Donald's *Charles Sumner and the Coming of the Civil War* (1965) and Robert J. Cook's *Civil War Senator: William Pitt Fessenden and the Fight to Save the American Republic* (2011).

Each of the three main authorities on the North's response to secession—Potter, Stampp, and McClintock—place Abraham Lincoln at the heart of the story. There is a vast literature on the nation's sixteenth president, some of it touching directly on the stale question of whether he was to blame for deliberately provoking civil war by attempting to resupply the federal garrison at Fort Sumter. This neo-Confederate argument was advanced most succinctly by Charles Ramsdell in his famous essay, "Lincoln and Fort Sumter," published in *The Journal of Southern History* in 1937. Owing to the work of Potter and Stampp, virtually all modern historians reject this one-sided thesis. However, there remains much debate about the extent to which Lincoln influenced events during the secession winter. Harold Holzer's *Lincoln President-Elect: Abraham Lincoln and the Great Secession Winter, 1860–1861* (2008) indicates that Lincoln was a far-from-passive actor during the crisis. The relevant chapters in Michael Burlingame's encyclopaedic two-volume *Abraham Lincoln: A Life* (2008) largely support this view. Nevertheless, Burlingame contends that Lincoln struggled to find a policy in March 1861, torn between Seward's war-avoidance strategy and his own desire to preserve the Union intact. Importantly, both Holzer and Burlingame make it clear that Lincoln was under enormous pressure during these weeks, not only from secessionists but also from Republican activists in general. Many of the latter were strong supporters of coercion and not a few were desperate for government jobs in the aftermath of their party's electoral triumph. Several fine single-volume biographies also probe Lincoln's actions and rhetoric during the secession crisis. These include David H. Donald's *Lincoln* (1995) and Richard Carwardine's *Lincoln: A Life of Purpose and Power* (2006).

The Confederate government, of course, was also deeply implicated in the outbreak of the American Civil War. The movements of Jefferson Davis's administration in the days and weeks leading up to the attack on Fort Sumter are assessed in two excellent biographies of the Southern president, William C. Davis's *Jefferson Davis: The Man and His Hour* (1991) and William J. Cooper, Jr.'s *Jefferson Davis, American* (2000). Good general histories of the Confederacy are also useful on this subject. See especially Emory M. Thomas's *The Confederate Nation: 1861–1865* (1979) and George C. Rable's *The Confederate Republic: A Revolution Against Politics* (2007). The South's bid for independence is set in global context by several of the contributors to Don H. Doyle's *Secession as an International Phenomenon: From America's Civil War to Contemporary Separatist Movements* (2010).

INDEX

1860 Association, 30
abolitionism/abolitionists, 14, 15, 39, 83; secessionist responses to, 3, 10–11, 25–26, 28, 30–31, 41, 67; Southern evangelicals' responses to, 17, 19, 20–21; and Southern grievance narrative, 72; stigmatized as disunionists, 36, 37–38, 56
Adams, Henry Brooks, 3
Adger, John, 22
African Americans, 21–22; and free blacks, 13, 61, 63. *See also* mulattoes; slavery; South; suffrage, black
African slave trade. *See* slavery: and slave trade, African
Alabama, 73
Alabama Baptist, 14
Alexandria Gazette, 44
American Colonization Society, 15
American Revolution. *See* memory
Anderson, Robert, 80
antislavery, Southern, 15–16, 18; political, 37, 38, 52
Appomattox, Confederate surrender at (1865), 57
Arkansas, secession of, 4
Arlington (Lee estate), 47, 55
Arnold, Benedict, 74

Baldwin, John B., 39
Baptists, 14, 15, 18, 21

Barlow, Samuel, 78
Bates, Edward, 62
Bell, John, 70
Beman, Nathan, 25–26
Bennett, James Gordon, 68
Blair, Francis Preston, 45, 62, 70, 76–77, 82
Blair, Montgomery, 62, 82, 83
Bledsoe, Albert Taylor, 55
Boston Herald, 79
Boston Massacre (1773), 61
Botts, John Minor, 37, 38, 41
Braddock, Edward, 65
Breckinridge, Robert J., 14
Brent, George, 38
Brevard, Keziah, 28
Brown, John, and Harpers Ferry raid (1859), 27, 40, 72, 73
Buchanan, James, 2, 15; administration of, 73, 75–76
Bunker Hill, Battle of (1775), 61, 64
Buzzard, Michael, 27

Calhoun, John C., 75
California, 74
Cameron, Simon, 61–62
capitalism, 5, 7
Charleston, S.C., 23, 30, 31
Charleston Mercury, 64
Charleston Southern Standard, 23
Chase, Salmon P., 81

Cheat Mountain, Battle of (1861), 55
Chesnut, James, 13
Chesnut, Mary, 17, 54
Chicago Daily Times and Herald, 77–78
Chicago Platform (1860), 89
Civil War, result of internal tensions, 2–3, 86–90
Clarke, Erskine, 19
Clay, Henry, 13–14, 36, 41; influence/legacy of, 37, 59, 81–82, 89
Cobb, Thomas R. R., 64–65, 67, 72
colonization, 13, 14, 15, 18, 59
Colyer, Mary Hancock, 70
commercial classes, 11, 30, 70, 78
Compromise of 1850, 74
Concord, Battle of (1775), 63
Confederacy, 2, 7, 88, 90; Congress of (1861), 54; Constitution of, 95n41; government of, 3, 4, 67–68, 84; Navy of, 46; occupation of U.S. property by, 80; and Revolutionary War memory, 67–68; seal of, 67; and secession of Virginia, 48, 52, 53–54
Constitutional Union Party, 70, 89
Continental Army, 63
Cornwallis, Earl, 66
correspondence, 34, 41, 42, 46, 51, 74, 96n1
cotton production, 13, 20
cotton states. *See* Lower South
Critcher, John, 49, 50
Crittenden, John J., compromise efforts by, 9, 76–78, 88, 89
Cuba, 77

Dabney, Robert Lewis, 20–21
Davis, Jefferson, 79; and compromise efforts, 74, 76; inaugural address of, 67, 88, 103n2; and Lee, 55; suggested as potential commander of Virginia armed forces, 48, 49–50
Declaration of Independence (1776), 67
Democratic Party, 15, 26, 39, 59, 68, 77, 80–81; and Breckinridge Democrats, 26; and Douglas Democrats, 7, 38, 48, 77–79,

89; national convention of, Charleston (1860), 25, 26; and Northern Democrats, 38, 75; and Southern Democrats, 13, 37, 38, 77, 79
diaries/journals, 1–2, 12, 16–17, 21, 27, 28, 54. *See also* Hurlbert, William Henry
disunion, 103n2; images of, 37–38; Northern, 37–38; Virginians' fear of, 36–37, 39–40, 41, 51–52, 56–57. *See also* secession
Douglas, Stephen A., 7, 15, 59, 75, 77, 78. *See also* fire-eaters: opposition to; Lincoln: Lincoln/Douglas debates
Dred Scott decision (1857), 67

Early, Jubal, 45, 49, 50, 56
Edmonds, Amanda, 27
elections, 3; of 1856, 39; of 1860, 15, 26, 68, 78, 89
emancipation, 17, 20–21, 32, 40, 86–87; gradual, 13, 14, 15, 21, 33
Europe, 5, 81
evangelicals, 12, 17–22, 25, 92n3

Far West, 76
Federalists, 43, 47, 75
fire-eaters, 3, 5, 12, 13, 23–26, 29–33, 37, 70; and compromise efforts, 72–74; and Cooperationists, 65–67; and defense of slavery, 23–26, 36–37, 40–41; and Lee, 34, 48–50; opposition of, to Douglas, 78–79; reaction of, to abolitionist rhetoric, 10–11; responses of, to Unionists, 7–8, 12–13, 39–41, 42, 51, 52–54, 56, 64–67, 85, 86–87; Unionist reactions to, 38–39
Floyd, John B., 55–56
forts, 4, 81; Fort Mason, 42; Fort Necessity, 65; Fort Pickens, 81; Fort Sumter, 4, 8, 43, 78, 82–83
Founding Fathers, 6; as embodiment of U.S. nationalism, 47–48; and legacy of "perpetual" Union, 42, 74; pro-slavery legacy of, 7–8, 47, 67. *See also* Jefferson, Thomas; Lincoln, Abraham: and view of Union; Madison, James; Washington, George

INDEX

Fox, Gustavus V., 84
free labor, 7
freesoilers, 39
French, Benjamin Brown, 1–2, 4, 89
French and Indian War (1756–63), 65
Fugitive Slave Act (1850), 37, 72, 75, 77–78
Fuller, Richard, 14–15

Gag Rule, attempts to repeal, 72
Garrison, William Lloyd, 37
George III, 65–66
Georgia, 19, 27, 52; Cooperationists in, 65; secession convention of, 53; state legislature of, 64–65, 67, 72
Great Britain, 5, 70
Greeley, Horace, 78

Haitian slave revolt (1791–1804), 62, 73
Halbwachs, Maurice, 60, 63
Hale, James T., 77
Hale, Stephen F., 73
Hall, Leonard S., 50
Hammond, James Henry, 12, 37
Hampton, Wade, II, 12
Hancock, John, 70
Harpers Ferry raid (1859), 27, 40, 72, 73
Hartford Convention (1814), 42
Hartley, L. P., 60
Harvie, Lewis, 48–50
Herndon, William H., 82, 83
Hill, Benjamin H., 65, 66
Hill, James L., 82–83
Holcombe, James, 73
Hughes, Henry, 24–25
Hurlbert, William Henry, 78, 79

Illinois, 81, 82–83
immigration/immigrants, European, 7, 15–16, 23, 63
Indiana, 77
intersectional tensions, 58, 86, 89–90; and Civil War causation, 4–5, 7–8, 9, 90; and collective memory, 71–80, 84; secessionists and, 28–29, 30–31, 33, 64–65

Jackson, Andrew, 36; administration of, 62; and nullification crisis (1832–33), 2, 75, 82, 83, 89
Janney, John, 47, 50, 51–52, 53
Jefferson, Thomas, 6, 7, 41, 47, 64
Jeffersonian Republican Party, 75
Jeter, Jeremiah, 18
Johnson, Andrew, 66, 68, 69, 80–81
Johnson, Marmaduke, 51
Johnston, James C., 11
Johnston, Joseph E., 48
Jones, Charles Colcock, 19–20
Jones, John G., 18
Jones, Mary, 19

Kansas, 73
Kansas-Nebraska Act (1854), 59, 75, 77, 100n3
Kemble, Fanny, 27
Kentucky, 6, 66, 73; Constitutional Convention of (1849), 14

Lee, Robert E., 6–7, 88, 89; appointment as Confederate general, 54; biographies of, 35–36, 47; as commander of Virginia armed forces, 48–51; conflicted over secession, 34–36, 41–48, 56; criticism of, 53, 55–57; and decision to leave Union, 35, 43–55, 97n18; military record of, 55–57; resignation of, from U.S. Army, 34; "Save in defense" pledge, 34–36, 42–43, 46, 52, 54–55, 57, 96n1; and sense of identity, 35; and state allegiance, 35, 47, 54–55, 57; as symbol of South, 56; and ties to Union, 36, 42–43, 57, 87; and view of secession, 41–42, 43–44, 57
Lee family: Anne, 96n1; Cassius, 45; Custis, 42; "Lighthorse" Harry, 44, 47, 52; Martha Custis Williams ("Markie"), 42, 96n1; Mary Custis, 45, 47; Rooney, 42; Sydney Smith, 45, 46, 96n1
Letcher, John, 48, 49, 50
Lexington, Battle of (1775), 63
Liberia, 14

Lincoln, Abraham, 65–66; administration of, 70, 87; and call for troops in 1861, 2, 4, 6–7, 44, 45, 46, 48, 50, 78, 89; and Clay, 81–82, 84, 89; Cooper Union speech of, 68; debates with Douglas, 26, 59; election of, as president, 64, 89; election of, Southern responses to, 11, 12, 16, 29–31, 32, 73; election of, triggers secession crisis, 1, 5, 33; and Fort Sumter crisis, 4, 61–62, 63, 79–85, 89; and historical memory, 81–84, 89; "House Divided" speech of, 39–40; and first inaugural, 60, 71, 80, 82, 83, 84; and Jackson, 83–84, 89; and nationalism, 83; Peoria speech of, 59; response of, to secession crisis, 38, 77, 85; and Seward, 79–81, 88–89; and slavery, 77, 80; and slavery extension issue, 59; and view of Union, 68, 71, 81, 83, 85

"Lost Cause" view of origins of Civil War, 56

Louisville, Ky., 14, 15

Louisville Examiner, 14

Lower South, 3, 5, 32–33, 86, 87; "coercion" of, 6–7; pro-slavery advocates in, 15–16; and secession/secessionists, 1, 38, 42, 53, 54; and slavery, 4, 87. *See also* Unionists

Lynchburg Virginian, 44, 54

Macfarland, William, 49, 50, 51, 54
Madison, James, 6, 41, 47, 58–59
Magoffin, Beriah, 73
Manigault, Charles, 32
Manly, Basil, Jr., 18
manumission, 18
Marshall, Anne, 46
Maryland, 66
Massachusetts, 38
Mayo, Joseph, 50
McClellan, George B., 56
memory: collective, 58–85, 90; and countermemories, 61; personal, 58, 59, 60, 61–63; Revolutionary War, 59, 60, 61, 63–71, 74, 84, 90; role of, in Civil War causation, 60–61, 84; selectivity of, 7–8, 73, 84–85. *See also* narratives

Methodism, 18

Mexican War (1846–48), 75

ministers/preachers, 12, 14, 17–22, 25–26, 31–32

Minute Men, 63

miscegenation, 12, 16–17, 87, 94n26

missionary work, 19, 22

Mississippi, 18, 67; Senate, 24

Missouri, 4, 15

Missouri Compromise (1820), 4, 9, 74, 75, 76–77

Monroe, James, 41

Montague, Robert, 40–41

Montgomery, Ala., 67, 103n2

Morning Courier and New-York Enquirer, 68

mulattoes, 16–17, 21–22

narratives: grievance, 7–8, 60, 71–80, 84–85, 90; Northern, 74–79, 84–85, 89; Southern, 60, 72–74, 85, 86–87. *See also* memory

nationalism, American, 6, 47, 56, 59, 64. *See also* Union, loyalty to

Newberry (S.C.) *Rising Sun*, 32–33

New Englanders, 42, 79

New Jersey Senate, 68

New Orleans, 15, 20, 31

New Orleans Bee, 11

New Orleans Daily Crescent, 74

New Orleans Daily Picayune, 72–73

New York, 25, 68, 69–70, 78, 81

New York Herald, 57, 68

New York Times, 78

Nicolay, John G., 83

Night, Melvina, 27

North, 55; economic resources of, 12, 29; internal tensions in, 4–5, 8, 9, 90; response of, to secession crisis, 1–2, 3–4, 7, 8, 68–71, 89. *See also* intersectional tensions; narratives; Republican Party

North Carolina, 16; secession of, 4

Nott, Josiah, 21–22

nullification crisis (1832–33), 58–59, 62

officeholders, 1, 13, 87; black, 87
Ohio, 8
Olmsted, Frederick Law, 16, 93n23

Palmer, Benjamin, 31–32
pamphlets, 30, 78–79; antislavery, 18; proslavery, 18; secession, 30, 32, 64
patriarchy, 5, 31–32
peace convention (1861), 2
Pendleton, James M., 14
Pennsylvania, 77
Peoria Daily Democratic Union, 79
Perry, Benjamin F., 11
Pettigrew, Caroline, 16, 32
Pettigrew, Charles, 16, 17
Philadelphia convention (1787), 1, 58
Phillips, Wendell, 83
Pierce, Franklin, administration of, 75–76
Pitt, William, the Elder, 71
planters, 6, 10, 11–12, 17, 18, 21, 23, 30; plantation wives, 16–17, 27, 94n26
political parties, 3, 6, 7, 90
Polk, James K., 75
Pollard, Edward, 56
polygenesis, 21–22
popular sovereignty, 59
Presbyterians, Old School, 14, 20–21, 25–26, 31–32
press, 55, 63; Northern, 74, 77, 79, 80; Southern, 32, 39, 44, 54, 56, 64, 97n18. *See also individual newspapers*
Preston, William C., 21
processions, 31, 50
propaganda, 30, 87. *See also* pamphlets
Pryor, Roger A., 40

Republican Party: as antislavery extremists, 7–8, 20, 37–38, 52, 67, 72–74; as Black Republicans, 5, 41, 87; as conservative Republicans, 1–2; formation of, 75, 100n3; and Founding Fathers' legacy, 8; as plotting Northern dominance, 6, 39–40, 44–45; response of, to secession crisis, 8, 62, 68–69, 76, 80, 81, 82–83, 88; Southern stigmatization of, 5, 6, 7–8, 20, 37–38, 39–40, 41, 44–45, 52, 67, 72–74, 87; support base, 15; and use of collective memory, 70–72, 74–79, 82–83, 84–85. *See also* Lincoln, Abraham
rhetoric: anti-abolitionist, 37; political, 3; pro-secession, 31–32, 40–41, 42, 53, 64–65, 72–74; pro-slavery, 92n3; pro-Union, 38–40, 42–43, 78–79
Rhett, Robert Barnwell, 12, 37, 64, 86
rice production, 13
Richardson, George, 41
Richmond, Va., 48, 50; Lee's defense of (1862), 56
Richmond Dispatch, 44, 54
Richmond Enquirer, 56
Richmond Examiner, 56
Ruffin, Edmund, 37
Russell, William Henry, 14

Saratoga, Battle of (1777), 63, 64
Scott, Winfield, 34, 43, 45, 46, 56, 84, 96n1
Sebastopol, siege of (1854–55), 62
secession, 1–2, 5, 86, 89; compromise efforts to avert, 2, 6, 7, 60, 72, 76–79, 84, 88; debates over, 64–67, 87–88; historical argument against, 68–69; psychological urge to secede, 8, 13; rationale for, 36; role of collective memory in, 60, 71–74; secession fever, 11–12, 16, 30–33; Southern views of, 11–12, 29, 33, 87–88; U.S. Cabinet responses to, 61–62. *See also* fire-eaters; Seward, William H.; Virginia
self-defense, creed of, and Virginia's secession, 47–48, 52, 54–55
Seven Days Battles (1862), 56
Seward, William H., 60; compromise efforts by, 3–4, 6, 70–71, 78, 88–89; "irrepressible conflict" speech of, 39–40, 86; as Secretary of State, 71, 77, 78, 79–80, 88–89
Sheffey, James W., 51
Sherman, John, 8
Sherman, William T., 8

"Slave Power," concept of, 3, 8, 75–77, 78, 84, 89

slavery, 16, 33, 86; claims for morality of, 23, 26, 31; defense of, 59, 92n3; defense of, religious, 12, 14–15, 17, 18, 20, 21, 22, 32; defense of, secular, 17, 21–22; extension of, 36, 64, 68, 72, 75–76, 87, 88; moral unease over, 5–6, 13–19, 25, 31–32, 33, 86, 92n3; Northern criticisms of, 7, 10–11, 26; and paternalism, 16, 18–19, 22, 24, 31, 32; reforms of, 92n3; and slave children, 94n26; and slave codes, 79; and slave families, 18, 19–20, 92n3; and slave numbers, 4, 13; and slave prices, 17, 20; and slave runaways, 32; and slaves sales, 19–20; and slave trade, African, 22, 23–25, 42, 74, 76, 95n41; and slave trade, domestic, 72; and slaveholders, 4, 18–19, 27, 36, 64–65, 87, 92n3; and slave-stealing, 67. *See also* Chicago Platform; Kansas-Nebraska Act; Missouri Compromise; planters; South: and fear of slaves

Slidell, John, 15

Smith, Benjamin Mosby, 21

Smith, William A., 15

South, 4, 56–57, 86; economy of, 6, 23, 28–29, 30–31, 59; and fear of slaves, 22, 24, 26–28, 32, 33, 39, 62, 86–87; and fear of slaves in response to Nat Turner's rebellion, 14, 73; internal tensions in, 3, 4–6, 8, 9, 13, 32–33, 86, 87, 90; and Southern conservatives, 10, 11–12, 33; and Southern moderates, 37, 54–55; and Southern nationalism, 55, 57, 90; and Southern rights, 12, 26, 50, 79; theme of self-respect in, 25–26, 30, 51; and view of North, 26, 28–29, 30–31, 33, 67, 72, 89; and view of Union as pro-slavery, 8, 53, 56–57. *See also* fire-eaters; Lower South; narratives; slavery; states' rights; Unionists; Upper South; Virginia

South Carolina, 22, 23, 25, 27, 29–30; disunionists in, 29; and nullification crisis (1832–33), 58–59, 75, 81–83; and ordinance of secession, 30; secession crisis in, 1–2, 11–12, 13, 29–33. *See also* Unionists

Southern Baptist Convention (1845), 14

Spratt, Leonidas W., 23–24, 95n41

state legislatures, Southern, 24, 25, 64–65, 67, 68, 72

states' rights, 11, 37, 47, 55, 57, 73, 74, 76; defenders of, 28–29. *See also* South: and Southern rights

Staunton Vindicator, 41

Stephens, Alexander H., 50, 51, 52–54, 65–66

Stringfellow, Thornton, 21

suffrage, black, 67, 87

sugar production, 13, 20

Summers, George W., 39

Sumner, Charles, 80

Taney, Roger B., 67

tariffs, 28, 58

Taylor, Richard, 16, 17, 93n23

Tea Party, 63

Tennessee, 14, 66, 75; secession of, 4

Texas, 43; annexation of, 75

Thomas, Ella Gertrude Clanton, 16–17, 94n26

Thornwell, James Henley, 22

Townsend, John, 29–30

Trenton, Battle of (1776), 68

Troy Daily Whig, 70

Tucker, Nathaniel Beverley, 37

Turner, Nat, rebellion (1831), 14, 62, 73

Tyler, John, 75, 81, 87, 88

Union: interpretations of, 37, 58–59; loyalty to, 63–64; Northern loyalty to, 2, 69, 70, 76, 90; Southern loyalty to, 6, 7, 34, 87. *See also* nationalism, American

Unionists, 1–2, 68; border-state, 71, 78; conditional (Southern), 6, 38–39, 41, 45, 49, 71, 88–89; Lower South, 11, 12–13, 29–30, 38; pro-slavery, 34, 36, 38, 72; Southern, 56, 79; Upper South, 44–45, 46, 71, 87–88; Virginia, 38–39, 40, 41, 42, 49, 50, 51, 66. *See also* nationalism, American

INDEX

Upper South, 4, 14, 53, 66, 80, 87, 88, 89; critics of slavery within, 13–15, 33; divisions with Lower South, 5–6, 13, 33; and nonseceding states, 3–4; and secession, 2, 4. *See also* Unionists

U.S. Army, 34, 43, 45, 46, 47

U.S. Congress, 3, 4, 23, 66, 72; and Committee of Thirteen (Senate), 77; and Committee of Thirty-three (House), 77; House of Representatives, 80; and secession crisis, 11; Senate, 12

U.S. Constitution, 67; and three-fifths clause, 74–75

Valley Forge, Pa., 63

vigilance committees, 27, 32

violence, white on black, 26–28, 32

Virginia, 6, 14, 15, 18, 21, 66, 80; attempts of, to influence secession crisis, 2, 39; economy of, 38–39, 40; historic influence of, 6, 39, 40–41, 42, 43–44, 59, 87, 89; political culture of, 6, 34, 36, 38–39, 41, 47–48; secession of, 4, 44–45; and secession convention, 34, 36, 38, 40–41, 42, 44–46, 48–54, 66, 73, 80; and states' rights advocates, 37; and union with Confederate states, 50, 52–54; and Virginia Resolution (1798), 58–59. *See also* Janney, John; Lee, Robert E.; Unionists

Walpole, Robert, 70

Ward, Sam, 78

War of 1812, 58

Washington, George, 6, 7, 64, 67; Virginians' reverence for, 41, 47, 48, 49, 51, 52

Wayland, Francis, 14–15

Webb, James Watson, 68–69

Webster, Daniel, 83; legacy of, 59

Weems, Mason Locke, 68

Whig Party, 59, 62, 70, 81, 89; nationalism of, 6, 43, 83; and slavery, 13–14; and Southern Whigs, 11, 37, 38, 45, 49, 65, 99

Willey, Waitman T., 39, 66, 68

Wilmot Proviso, 72

Wilson, Henry, 78

Wise, Henry A., 15, 41, 45, 50, 51, 56, 78

women. *See* planters: plantation wives

Yancey, William Lowndes, 25–26, 78, 86

Yates, Richard, 83

Yorktown, Battle of (1781), 63, 64

www.ingramcontent.com/pod-product-compliance
Lightning Source LLC
Chambersburg PA
CBHW030401170426
43202CB00010B/1452